SUBMARINE UPHOLDER

Sydney Hart

AMBERLEY PUBLISHING

First published 2008

Amberley Publishing Plc
Cirencester Road, Chalford,
Stroud, Gloucestershire, GL6 8PE

www.amberley-books.com

British Library Cataloguing in Publication Data.
A catalogue record for this book is available from the British Library.

ISBN 978 1 84868 116 3

Typesetting and Origination by diagrafmedia
Printed in Great Britain

CONTENTS

INTRODUCTION

To the average civilian the British Submarine Service is one cloaked in mystery; the names of its heroes – and there were many – practically unknown. The exploits of our most famous undersea craft only half-told. But at the annual reunions of the Submarine Service, at Fort Blockhouse, Gosport, home of the whole organisation, all submariners re-live their memories for they are 'home' again. They drink their toasts to 'The Queen', 'Absent friends', and 'Submariners still on Patrol', meaning the many, alas, who never returned. Over seventy of these deadly warcraft were lost in the Second World War; more than forty in the Mediterranean, the background of this story.

This is the account of one such submarine: H.M. Submarine Upholder and her captain Lieutenant-Commander Malcolm David Wanklyn, V.C., D.S.O. (two bars), who is recognised in the Service as the greatest of all submariners. Also of the crew, whom he led so gallantly.

H.M.S. Upholder destroyed one-eighth of a million tons of enemy shipping in sixteen months. During one single patrol she sank 40,000 tons: ships that were crammed with troops *en route* to the stark battlefields of North Africa, or supplies to maintain them in the field: surely a deciding factor in the results of the vital North African campaign. In addition she accounted for three U-boats and one destroyer. Two cruisers and one destroyer also felt the sting of her torpedoes, even if they did not find final port on the Mediterranean's bottom.

An original painting of this heroic officer hangs in the 'Whispering Gallery' of Fort Blockhouse: a gallery in the submarine officers' wardroom enriched with the photographs of submarines which have long since served their purpose and achieved honourable retirement-either to the scrapheap or to the seas, whose depths they employed as their field of victory. It is a gallery of proud memories, and Wanklyn's portrait is in its rightful place amongst the reproductions of the vessels he loved.

In the Base church a font bears his name: it is there in his memory, to do him honour; he who never wilfully sought honour but only victory for the service of his choice. How many future submariners will be baptised here it is impossible to say, but undoubtedly they will receive inspiration from such a sacrament.

The Submarine Service will never forget this great man. But what does the non-submariner know of his deeds?

The Submarine Service is undoubtedly the most economical of all the armed forces of the Crown. It is also the hardest-hitting force, and I am sure that all readers will agree with me – after reading this book – that, man for man, pound sterling for pound sterling, no other service played such a part in bringing the nation's enemies to their knees.

It is my wish that this book will help, in some small way, to get the great British public submarine-minded.

We have the finest submariners in all the world, so let us have the finest submarines, and let them be a memorial to such men as David Wanklyn and the heroes who served under him, together with all submariners 'still on patrol'. We can be assured that the modern British submariner in this age of nuclear propulsion is worthy of the highest perfection in atomic submarine construction. He is the best-trained specialist in the world.

One has but to see a part of the strenuous, meticulous training he has to undergo to realise this. Take a peep at his training today: see him in the escape tank, 100 feet deep; see him making a dare-devil escape from a supposedly wrecked submarine, with 100 feet of water between him and safety. He climbs out of his underwater compartment without any mechanical aids, with 45 lb. per square inch of water-pressure on him. He rises slowly through the deep water with only the air in his lungs to assist him, and a nose-clip to protect his nostrils, breathing out through the mouth to balance the pressures as he ascends. This is just a small part of his training, but enough to make a spectator realise just the type of superman who helps to crew our submarines.

I am deeply grateful to the following for their invaluable assistance in the compilation of this work: Mrs. Elspeth Wanklyn, his wife; Mrs.

Marjorie Wanklyn, Lieutenant-Commander Wanklyn's mother; Miss Joan Wanklyn, his sister. Too, I wish to include my old C.O. of H.M. submarine *Thrasher*, Captain H. S. Mackenzie, R.N., D.S.O. and Bar, D.S.C.; Commander M. L. C. Crawford, R.N., D.S.C. and Bar, who was First Lieutenant in H.M. submarine *Upholder* for many patrols; Mr. F. G. Selby, D.S.M. and Bar, *Upholder's* Second Coxswain; the entire staff at Fort Blockhouse; Lieutenant-Colonel R. Wilson, D.S.O. and Bar, T.D. (Special Service attached to Submarines) for the account of *Upholder's* last patrol.

My sincere thanks are also extended to Mr. E. Hepworth and Mr. E. Holly, of the Admiralty Record Office, for the willing assistance given to me.

In conclusion, my gratitude to My Lords Commisioners of the Admiralty, for their consent to my inspection of the documents dealing with *Upholder's* incredible career.

SYDNEY HART

CHAPTER 1

MALCOLM DAVID WANKLYN

SUBMARINE *Upholder's* crew stood or sat around at the Lazaretto Submarine Base at Malta on 6 April 1942. At their feet were their small canvas steaming-bags. Alertly the coxswain watched. This was the last few minutes before he called: 'Harbour Stations'.

With that extra sense that was an integral part of all coxswains he knew the moment to make the call.

'All aboard, lads.'

Feet thudded on the floating catwalk between *Upholder* and the shore, and then clanged on her steel casing. The men disappeared below to their appointed stations.

Last aboard was the tall, bearded figure of her Commanding Officer, Lieutenant-Commander Malcolm David Wanklyn, V.C., D.S.O. (two bars), now a legendary name in the Mediterranean.

Preceding him were three incongruous figures, one battledress-clad, the others were Arabs.

The First Lieutenant saluted, Wanklyn returned the salute.

'All ready for sea, sir.'

'Thank you, Number One.'   '

After a few minutes. 'Slow ahead. Port.' Then, 'Slow ahead, starboard.' Switches were rammed home in a shower of sparks in the motor-room. The water boiled around her stern, the gap between her and the shore slowly widened. She moved away gathering speed toward the harbour entrance.

'Good luck, David,' came faintly over the water from the Base. Wanklyn acknowledged it with a wave. Then the open sea, a trim dive to Wanklyn's satisfaction and submarine *Upholder*, 630 tons of lethal menace, was open to business.

Her passengers were Captain R. A. (Tug) Wilson, Royal Artillery, and two native agents whom *Upholder* had to put ashore in North Africa.

And of *Upholder*? This was her twenty-fifth patrol. In twenty-four patrols she had destroyed rather more than an eighth of a million tons of enemy shipping, including three U-boats. She had denied Rommel and his then all-conquering Afrika Korps vital supplies and much needed reinforcements. She had turned parts of the Italian and Sicilian coast into graveyards so that nervous enemy captains saw in every breaking wave a periscope, in every line of froth on the sea a lethal torpedo.

Upholder put Captain Wilson and his cloak-and-dagger men ashore. Wilson returned to *Upholder* and transferred to submarine *Unbeaten* to return to Gibraltar.

Upholder swung away to start her main task, the patrolling of the western approaches to Tripoli to sink such of His Majesty's enemies as she encountered. That was 11 April.

On the 12th Captain 'Shrimp' Simpson, Captain Submarines, ordered submarines *Upholder*, *Urge* and *Thrasher* to establish a patrol line to intercept a valuable convoy bound for Tripoli early on 15 April.

But, on 14 April *Urge* and *Thrasher* – on which I was serving – heard the thump of depth-charging. *Thrasher* was next to *Upholder* in the patrol line and we could hear the prolonged din without the aid of asdic.

Later contact was made with *Urge*. We tried to make a link with *Upholder* at 8.30 p.m. on 14 April – and failed. Again the next day we tried. And again we failed.

From then onwards nothing was heard from *Upholder*. The rest is conjecture. Had the powerful escort to the convoy trapped *Upholder*? Deluged her with an unceasing storm of depth-charges?

Nobody will ever know with certainty.

But *Upholder* and her Commanding Officer, David Wanklyn and his crew lie somewhere off the Tripoli coast joining many others for whom there is no marked grave.

Apart from the author's personal opinion of David Wanklyn's outstanding quality, it is more than confirmed by extracts from official letters as included below.

The Rt. Hon. A. V. Alexander, First Lord of the Admiralty, in a commendatory letter to Mrs. Wanklyn, quotes the commendation of

Captain G. W. G. Simpson, R.N., who commanded the Malta Submarine Flotilla to which *Upholder* belonged, to the following effect:

> I hope it is not out of place to take this opportunity of paying some small tribute to Lieutenant-Commander David Wanklyn, V.C., D.S.O. two bars, and his Company in H.M.S. *Upholder*, whose brilliant record will always shine in the records of British submarines, and the history of the Mediterranean Fleet in this war.
>
> ... A personal friend who had been my First Lieutenant in peace time and latterly, during service from Malta, a particularly valuable adviser on all operational matters, it seems to me that Wanklyn was a man that the nation can particularly ill afford to lose.
>
> His modesty, determination and exceptionally fine character made aim a natural leader, who received automatically the loyalty and maximum effort from all who served with him. As an example of this, during the past year, two or three worthless scamps have been drafted to *Upholder*, never again to appear at the Defaulters' table. Wanklyn had exceptional intellectual ability and judgment far beyond his years.
>
> I am glad to think that in January I asked him if he would not like to return to the United Kingdom, since I thought he looked tired, to which he replied that it was his ambition to return to the United Kingdom in command of *Upholder*. In February he stood off one patrol and in March operated *Upholder* with his usual brilliance. After this he asked me if the docking of *Upholder* could be changed with another submarine so that he could remain on the station a further two months, and 'add to his bag', which I refused.

Admiral Sir Henry Harwood (of Battle of River Plate fame) when Commander-in-Chief Mediterranean, in forwarding Captain Simpson's report, added that

> H.M.S. *Upholder's* brilliant career was an inspiration, not only to the Mediterranean Fleet, but to the people of Malta as well....

The First Lord of the Admiralty added:

> I personally, and all my colleagues on the Board of Admiralty, fully endorse these tributes to the memory of an Officer whose character and exploits will serve as an example and inspiration to the Service for many years to come.

Admiral (S) R. B. Darke wrote to Mrs. Wanklyn

> ... Your husband was gifted with qualities given only to great men, the chief
> among which is inspiration followed by modesty in the face of great and
> conspicuous success. He had these qualities among many others in abundance
> and exercised them to the benefit of all with whom he came in contact. The
> greatest tribute that could be paid to him was paid to him by his brother
> commanding officers, peers themselves at their jobs, who recognised and
> regarded him as something above them all, yet one who set an example which
> all could and wanted to emulate, but few could hope to achieve ...

What manner of man was this Malcolm David Wanklyn who in the
space of less than two years was awarded the V.C. and three D.S.O.'s, in
a service which is notoriously slow to go into lavish praise for even a job
well done?

And what manner of ship was this?

Take the man first.

Wanklyn was born at the Hermitage, Alipore, Calcutta, to William
Lumb Wanklyn and his wife Marjorie on 28 June 1911. His father was a
consulting engineer and partner in the firm of Andrew Yule & Company,
later Yule, Gatto & Company.

Contrary to general opinion David Wanklyn was not a Scot. He loved
Scotland and permitted the legend to continue in circulation that he was
a Scot. But, his father was English and his mother was Irish for several
generations back.

She was a great lover of horses, and as a young woman had a wonderful
pair of hands, delicate, but firm and with that touch which is difficult to
describe but is easily recognised. It would appear that she passed on that
attribute to her son.

There is little naval background in his family, at least not in the
immediate circle, but his love of the Navy came through a chance
meeting, a cousin who commanded a destroyer in the First World War.

At the outbreak of the war in 1914 his father came home to join the
Army – and brought his family with him. He settled them in Moynes Court,
Chepstow, and went off to serve. David Wanklyn was then three and a half.
Toward the close of the war a British destroyer rammed and sank a German
submarine off the Irish coast. To have the damage repaired she was sent to
Newport, only a few miles from Chepstow. And one of her officers was a

cousin of Wanklyn's. In a cousinly way this naval officer called at Moynes Court. David and his mother were walking in the garden when suddenly they came face to face with the young officer. The seed was sown.

David and his mother were invited to visit the ship and from that moment onwards there was not the slightest deviation in his ambition. Whenever he was asked what he was going to do his prompt answer was: 'I'm going into the Navy, of course.'

He was eminently an outdoor boy, especially good with horses with the inherited touch for them handed on from his mother.

He was a fearless climber, trees or rocks, but it was a calculated fearlessness, risks assayed and accepted. An example will serve. While living with his parents at Knockinaam, Ayrshire, his mother would lead David and his three brothers in wild scrambles over the rocks.

She would look at a tall tree, or a challenging towering rock, and would cry: 'Now, who's going up that?'

The four boys would leap at the obstacle, but with David there would be a moment of analysis – then he would be racing for the top like a scorched baboon, all risks calculated. Risk, calculated and accepted, was the be-all and end-all of his too brief career.

Again, an example of his touch with horses. All animals went well for him and it is an accepted tenet that a man who can handle horses can invariably handle men.

Of the four brothers he was the only one who could ride *Noel*, a grey part-Arab hunter belonging to his mother. Like all horses with a strong strain of Arab in them, *Noel* was a mixture of high spirits and near hysterical temperament. For David's mother, *Noel* would 'go'. For David's brothers, *Noel* would become a whirlwind with a dash of typhoon injected into him. For David, *Noel* would become controlled, dynamic power.

There is an old Service saying: 'You may be a good horse, but there are plenty of jockeys to ride you.'

It explains itself. In the years to follow plenty of naval ratings discovered in David Wanklyn a sure-fire winning jockey!

In his early days his health was not of the best, perhaps the change from the blood-thinning heat of India to the harsher climate of Britain had something to do with it.

Wisely his parents decided against any molly-coddling and allowed an active, open-air life to build for him an ultimate sound constitution because in later years there was not a suspicion of weakness about him either physical or mental. He could, and did, find hidden reserves and appeared to be nowhere near exhaustion point under conditions which found other men on the verge of collapse.

Yet, with it all, outside his own family circle he was a shy boy. At his prep school he was known as 'Mouse'. The DAY for which he waited came slowly nearer, on dragging feet, but eventually came. He completed the written examination required for entry into the Royal Naval College, Dartmouth, then had to face the Selection Board.

It is the fashion to picture the Senior Officers on this Board as men with gin-purpled faces, anxious only to know if one's mother has ever entertained admirals to dinner and if one's father belongs to the best clubs.

It is as arrant a piece of fiction as the chinless curate. Senior Officers of an Admiralty Selection Board are men who have sailed the long hard course and know what they are looking for. Not an intellectual brilliance at thirteen-plus years old – that is a flame which can die to a dim smoulder at twenty and be a cold torch at twenty-five.

What was looked for was some evidence of common sense, some evidence of power of leadership, an ability to think. Even though the qualities were only in an embryo form the Board welcomed evidence of them. The Navy would bring them to maturity.

And in Malcolm David Wanklyn they found them because in January 1925, at the age of thirteen years and a few months, he entered the Royal Naval College, Dartmouth, as a cadet.

In those days the Navy firmly believed in getting them young!

At Dartmouth he was in the St. Vincent term. Some of his shyness still remained, in fact it remained with him until the end of his days.

There is not much scope for individuality in the first year or two at Dartmouth. It is not discouraged so long as it is not in a wildly misfitting boy seeking refuge from the hurly-burly of an establishment not famed for its tenderness. But David Wanklyn did develop an individual hobby – in fact it was more, it became a passion. He became an ardent bird-watcher. That hobby demanded intense observation and endless patience, traits which served him well in his later career.

Not that he shirked the more conventional fun and games of the College. His light, wiry frame never seemed to tire and he was a more than passable whipper-in of the college beagles. By no means a sinecure, at least not the way the R.N.C. beagles were hunted!

Nothing helps more in forming a boy's character than messing about in boats. A boy can make a mistake through carelessness when riding a bicycle and get up with nothing more than a few scratches and a buckled wheel as evidence of his lack of forethought. He can take a chance on a pony's back and find himself dumped on to the hard ground with a few more bruises to both his body and his pride.

But, make a mistake in a boat under canvas and there is every chance of that error becoming a multiple tragedy. David Wanklyn messed about in boats – and learned. When his parents paid their occasional visits to Dartmouth, he would meet them at Kingswear and instead of allowing them to use the ordinary ferry from Kingswear to Dartmouth he would insist on sailing them across, confident that, with his precious passengers with him, he could meet any normal contingency.

There was a short, intensive period of introspection. He decided that he would be top cadet of his term, not from vanity, but to satisfy himself that he was capable of producing the qualities he felt were necessary to his chosen career.

Most boys at one period or another, perhaps prodded by an anguished conscience, suffer from this inner analysis – then they punt a rugger ball around and they forget it.

Not David Wanklyn.

He drove himself like a nigger at the tasks set him. This misdirected zeal brought the inevitable retribution. He began to run a succession of temperatures and finally had to go to hospital and during that period of enforced idleness he had time to reconsider and replan his ideas.

During his time at the College the system of two watches was current. The cadets were divided into port and starboard watches and a persistent rivalry between port and starboard was encouraged. It required from the boys an individual application and a collective effort.

David Wanklyn decided that so far as he was concerned his effort would materially help his watch.

It was through constant unflagging application that he passed out of Dartmouth after four years with five firsts, top of the list in five subjects. It may not be a record, but for a boy who never claimed to possess sheer brilliance it was certainly nothing to be ashamed of.

So, on the first of May 1929 he was gazetted midshipman and was entitled to wear the white lapel patches of that rank. His first sea-going ship was *Marlborough*, and once again he found himself the most junior boy.

He had progressed from a thirteen- and-a-half-year-old, brand-new cadet at Dartmouth to the dizzy, heady heights of a senior with all the privileges.

Now he was at the bottom of another ladder with but one foot on the rung.

There was study galore and occasional trim in command of a picket boat with a sympathetic coxswain at the wheel to temper either timidity or brash overconfidence on coming alongside with a critical officer at the head of the gangway.

After rather more than a year on *Marlborough*, a year of work and of ceremonial when she visited foreign ports, advertising the power and might of the British Navy, he was appointed to the first-class battle-cruiser *Renown*.

With a score of other youngsters in the gunroom David Wanklyn stood the risk of becoming a nonentity, an average dogsbody. Is it unreasonable to assume that it was then the kernel of thought came to him that in small ships there was more scope for the individualist?

A year on Renown saw him receive the rank of Sub-Lieutenant with attendant long courses of instruction to enable him to qualify for his second ring as a full lieutenant.

A man of resourcefulness, capable of coping with an emergency coolly and calmly, a man with a power of command, and that at an age when public schoolboys of the conventional type are beginning to worry whether they will get their school colours or not!

Those courses took him to various 'stone frigates'; Whale Island for gunnery, Greenwich for navigation, many places in fact where useful information might be gleaned.

During this period of intensive study, his father, to whom he was devoted, died. His mother, realising that the news of this fatality would disturb her son's mind and distract him from the close study necessary to triumphant success, informed the C.O. of the College and left it to his personal discretion whether to pass on the sad news of his bereavement or not. Very wisely, the Senior Officer kept David in the dark until the exams were passed satisfactorily, though his subsequent grief can best be left to the imagination.

Granted three months' leave, Wanklyn proved to be of invaluable assistance to his bereaved mother. He was very good with children, and his fondness for his younger brother and sister brought their consequent adoration. David applied himself to the task of easing his sister's grief by instructing her in the use of the variety of tools in his father's workshop. Being a good model-maker he soon managed to absorb her interest, and also won her enthusiastic interest in stamp-collecting.

Within four months he was confirmed in Sub-Lieutenant's rank; after one year he was made a Lieutenant and given a good deal of authority. He was now qualified for a small independent command, if he aspired to such dignity. But within a few months of securing the second ring he applied for the 'service inside the service' – submarining aboard H.M.S. *Dolphin*, Fort Blockhouse – which involved an intensified three months' training in the subjects likely to make a good under-water expert.

This course was demanding, with no favours shown, in particular the escape courses which were practical in the extreme.

To be sure, the idea of practical escape seldom enters a submariner's mind; some trainees might consider such courses a mere matter of routine, quite unnecessary. But David went through them with a dogged determination to do his best; exactly the spirit that had actuated his earlier efforts since joining the Service. He wasn't content with learning how things should be done: he wanted to know WHY.

The escape instructors were more than highly qualified to impart worth-while information. Whilst acting under the overall command of the officer detailed for the purpose, they were individualists enough to accept responsibility on their own account, especially in case of emergency – which occasionally happened.

First then, the trainees were instructed in the theory of the necessary breathing-sets: this was a classroom job and as thorough as such a vital bit of tuition should be. These breathing sets are as nearly foolproof as human ingenuity can devise, and they need a man of intelligence to operate them – a man of cool, unscarable level-headedness. Naturally only such types are accepted for the submarine service; the examining medical officers see to that.

From the escape course Wanklyn graduated to the officers' course in submarine work proper, classrooms for what seemed endless hours of theory with an occasional break from confining walls.

On these courses officers seem to divide themselves into two classes or types. There is the one type who closes his book once the clock shows the time for the end of study. There is the other type who spends a lot of his own time swopping notes with fellow officers, casting back over his books and papers. Still learning.

Is it so odd that those who do that seem to forge ahead of the types who prefer to hold their analysis of the course propped against the bar of the junior Officers' Club with a pink gin in their hands.

There are seldom many of that type in a course and time finds them out. The Submarine Service, above all others in the Navy, demands dedication – and gets it.

But it was not all class work, important as that was.

Occasional day-trips aboard the training submarine were arranged which inculcated the practical application of all the details learned in Stokes Bay; and this approximated the real thing, though the submarine employed might not have been the last word in modern construction. The idea was to give David and his fellows the feel of a submarine, and the confidence so necessary to one who desires to become a top-liner at his chosen trade. He became aware of the characteristic smell of a submarine. There is no other smell quite like it: it has the same effect on a veteran submariner as the smell of Stockholm tar has on an ancient windjammer sailor. This characteristic smell has a compelling effect on the beginner – it makes him wish to become part of it – to steep himself in the spirit of the Submarine Service, almost as if it were a pep-drug.

Finally he underwent the double passing-out exam, written and oral, after which he qualified – with credit, needless to say, as a competent Submarine Officer, even if in a junior rank.

In September, 1933, he received his appointment to H.M. submarine *Oberon*, a large, ungainly under-water craft, which was fairly up to date and an adequate ship in which to continue his training.

After a brief period in *Oberon* he went to L.56 and then onwards to the trial horse, H.50, to which he was appointed First Lieutenant. This submarine was old, cramped and very small, lacking nearly all the improvements to be found in more modern submarines. But she was eminently suitable for breaking in a First Lieutenant whose all-embracing duties ranged from store supervision, discipline, father confessor to the ratings, to controlling the ship's driving trim. A hundred feet was her diving limit – with safety – and she was as delicate as a scientist's scales. A trial horse indeed and one to detect the ham-handed in double-quick time.

In less than a year, now dedicated to submarines, he was appointed to H.M. submarine *Sea Lion*, an S-class boat, larger and more up to date than the H-class submarines. Then onwards, after three months to

Shark (another S-class) still as First Lieutenant and still broadening his experience out in the Mediterranean. And he fell in love!

The object of his affections was a cool, calm canny Scots girl, Elspeth Kinloch. They met at a picnic. So far as he was concerned a few seconds was long enough for him to know that Elspeth Kinloch was the ONE woman for him.

But, being a canny Scots girl she wanted to have more time to think it over. Was it love for her? Or was it just the Malta moon?

She returned home, and by an odd little twist of fate *Shark* was sent home also for a refit.

They met again and this time Elspeth had no doubts. She, too, was in love.

Shark's refit was completed in far too quick a time for Wanklyn and she was ordered back to Malta.

At that time the war clouds, although but still only darkening the horizon, were looming blackly. Leave to England, even for such an important thing as marriage, was uncertain. They decided to be married in Malta and in May 1938 the ceremony took place in Holy Trinity, Sliema, with the reception held on the submarine parent ship, *Resource*.

Taormina, that lovely Sicilian resort, was chosen for the honey moon. This was the year of Munich, when the dictators were riding high. Mussolini had completed his infamous conquest of Abyssinia and was giving raucous tongue to his ambitions.

Although on honeymoon Wanklyn kept his eyes wide open and was constantly making notes of any salient features, notes of anything in the way of landmarks which might prove of value to a submarine officer who in turn might be operating off that coast in the grim trade of war.

Elspeth Wanklyn accepted the somewhat harsh conditions – even in times of peace – under which a naval officer's wife was required to live. There were the long absences, together with the ever-present risks of the Submarine Service.

In one respect she reformed him, mellowed him, taught him how to unbend. A naturally shy man, he hid behind an impeccable behaviour even on social occasions when senior officers were present. But gradually he was brought to realise that other junior officers and their wives, were more relaxed, were on less formal terms with the Brass. Gradually, under her subtle tuition he overcame, in some degree, his shyness, and later, when he himself became a senior officer he allowed quite a lot of latitude to his juniors which made for good feeling all round.

Had he lived, and had he reached high rank, as he would undoubtedly have done, Wanklyn would have readily admitted his debt to the woman he married.

In September 1938, while Chamberlain was buying valuable time at Munich, Wanklyn and his wife came home to spend his foreign leave in the Scotland he loved and in November he was appointed to submarine *Porpoise* which was then commanded by 'Shrimp' Simpson. They were to meet later when 'Shrimp' Simpson was Captain (S) of the Malta submarines. It was the beginning of a firm friendship and mutual understanding between the men – both of whom had marked qualities.

In July 1939 he was appointed spare submarine officer at *Dolphin* and his wife took a furnished house at Havant. The birth of their first child was due in a few weeks.

Then Wanklyn was appointed First Lieutenant of *Otway* under orders to proceed forthwith to the Mediterranean.

He sailed with mixed feelings.

On 31 August their son Ian was born and Elspeth Wanklyn was still convalescent when on Sunday, 3 September, Chamberlain's weary voice announced that we were at war.

This was followed almost immediately by the first banshee wail of the siren. Elspeth held her newborn child close to her. What did the Great Unknown hold for her? Would the bombs fall on them? And where was her husband, now at war?

It was five weeks before Wanklyn received a cable telling him of the birth of his son, such were the exigencies of war in its early days.

He was doing shakedown trials and patrols in Mussolini's *Mare Nostrum* where no shooting war existed – for the time being.

Submarine *Otway* returned to England in December 1939 for David Wanklyn to see his first-born and to start a course for commanding officers, perhaps not in that order but that is how they were valued by the Wanklyn family.

He commanded H.31 and H.32, obsolete First World War submarines and ran asdic target for surface ships working from Portland.

So heavy were our submarine losses in those first few months of what some cynic labelled 'the phoney war' that until the building lag was caught up those old subs. had to go into active service. Wanklyn took H-31 to Blyth and did several North Sea patrols in her.

In August 1940 he was appointed to submarine *Upholder*, then merely a job number in a Barrow shipyard. He got accommodation for his wife and son and stood by his new ship as she was being built, the latest and the best of everything was to go into her.

He watched her grow from a gaunt, red rusted skeleton, took a lively and expert interest in her construction, at times relying on charm of manner to smooth the ruffled feelings of dockyard experts who might have felt that his insistent demands were occasionally a nuisance.

His constant theme was: 'You are building her, but I have to take her to sea and fight with her, so could I PLEASE have it my way?'

In most instances he got his way.

Like most men who go down to the sea in ships Wanklyn was a Christian, even though he might have described God as 'Somebody up there' – a militant Christian, of the brand of Cromwell's Ironsides, but with it all a gentle man with complete control of his temper.

Thus is completed the picture of Malcolm David Wanklyn, a dedicated man.

CHAPTER 2

UPHOLDER IN COMMISSION

Now what of the ship?

Upholder was not one of the largest type of submarines; she was designed for killing in coastal waters, for killing along the enemy's coast!

She was 630 tons displacement, not differing greatly from other under-water craft in appearance. She was 196 feet long with a beam of 12 feet, a venomous shark of a ship. Her surface speed was 12 knots, diving speed to below periscope depth was about 45 seconds and her submerged speed was 9 knots. Her maximum depth was 200 feet, not anywhere near as deep as the maximum depths achieved by larger submarines. But she was built for working in coastal waters.

This slim, lethal lance carried eight 21-inch torpedoes, four at the 'ready' in her tubes and four re-loads. Each torpedo's war-head carried 1,000 pounds of high explosive capable of blowing in the side of a tough ship.

The torpedoes were ejected from the tubes by compressed air and once under way electric motors took over the propulsion. The average cost of a torpedo was around £3,000, not toys to be lightly thrown away at indifferent targets.

Her armament consisted of one 12-pounder gun mounted for'ard of the conning tower. On top of this tower was the small bridge which when she was surfaced generally held the officer of the watch, two for'ard look-outs, and the after look-out. With the commanding officer 'up top' as well it was rather crowded and moving about was akin to doing a tango in a telephone box.

In one respect she differed from most submarines. Her ballast tanks, on which a submarine dives, went clean around the bottom instead of being merely at the sides. This gave her good stability for diving instead of making her prone to listing to one side when submerging as so often happened in submarines with only the side ballast tanks.

Her complement was thirty-two, four officers and twenty-eight other ranks and ratings.

After the inevitable and seemingly endless delays *Upholder*, still a job number, was launched. Unfortunately, on that day Mrs. Wanklyn was confined to her bed with a sharp and depressing bout of influenza.

No longer a number, but named, *Upholder* was commissioned and eventually was ready for trials. Her crew had been gradually assembling at Barrow, first the key men, then the remainder, and in that respect *Upholder* was fortunate. Most of her men were regular submariners with only a slight leavening of 'hostility men'.

With the builder's men still on board *Upholder* went to Gareloch for diving trials before Wanklyn could finally accept the ship.

She was trimmed down to conning tower depth, then periscope depth, then 70 feet and finally came the emergency test. The air screamed into the ballast tanks and *Upholder* rose swiftly to the surface like a whale coming up from a deep plunge in a bubbling whirl of broken water.

Wanklyn signed the acceptance chit and assumed responsibility for the ship. He was then a twenty-nine-year-old lieutenant.

Once the ship was his there followed working-up trials – diving off the klaxon, a crash dive in more dramatic parlance, instant readiness, mock attacks, gun actions, everything that could knit men and ship into an efficient fighting mechanism.

In peace-time this can be a leisurely procedure, with much care given to doing it in slow time first and quickening the pace later.

In war-time it was concentrated. Submarines were wanted urgently.

During trials at Gareloch there was still time for a little relaxation. Whilst ashore, Wanklyn, on a shooting expedition, shot a hare. Back in *Upholder* he decided to have the hare jugged. Able Seaman Young, the sub.'s gunlayer and cook was put in charge of the jugging operation. For several days the hare hung in *Upholder's* galley till it was nice and strong – much to the crew's discomfort (during that spell the submarine was doing day runs in connection with trials).

At the end of one day's run *Upholder* tied up alongside the submarine depot ship *Forth*. Able Seaman Young decided that now was the time and the place to clean the hare. It was now smelling so strongly that he had to take the thing on the after-casing (deck). Unfortunately for Young, *Upholder's* after-casing was in line with the cabin of Captain Submarines. In fact he was gutting the stinking hare beneath the Captain's porthole. In a few seconds an angry Captain (S) was bawling at Young wanting to know what the devil was happening. It's impossible to find out what happened to the hare.

Eventually Wanklyn was more or less satisfied and shortly a signal was received ordering him to proceed to Portsmouth.

During these trials Wanklyn had been growing a prideful submariners' beard. When she came south Wanklyn arranged to meet his mother in the foyer of a restaurant for a mild celebration and a farewell. She sat there among the throng of people, expectant, and spared a glance or two for the tall, bearded young officer who also seemed to be waiting. Finally he turned his back and she recognised him from the back of his head!

At Fort Blockhouse, Gosport, Wanklyn's temporary First Lieutenant departed and his place was taken by Lieutenant M. L. C. Crawford. Wanklyn and Crawford had met briefly in the Mediterranean. Crawford was experienced, although not in the type of ship of *Upholder*, but Wanklyn liked him, in fact it was mutual.

Nothing official had been said about her sphere of operations, but submariners are knowledgeable men and shrewdly guessed that the place for a submarine of *Upholder's* type would be the Mediterranean. The news from there was far from encouraging. Losses in under-water craft were considerable. It was only on the stage of a variety hall that the Italian Navy could be ridiculed. Its pursuit craft were fast and efficient and deadly as our mounting losses showed.

Ultimately it came. 'Being in all respects ready for sea... .' And it was the Mediterranean.

She sailed on 10 December 1940.

A December passage to Gibraltar is no picnic in any class of ship and *Upholder* was, after all, only a small ship of just over 600 tons.

She rolled and pitched into the high vicious Bay of Biscay seas, lively as a piece of driftwood, and most of her crew, although experienced seamen, paid tribute to Neptune.

On that passage *Upholder* had her first troubled incident.

There is not much room on a U-class submarine. In hard weather the air becomes vitiated in the cramped space. The hull, with its inherent elasticity, develops a play. This caused one of the watertight doors, a heavy mass of metal, to spring off the holding clip.

Chief Engine Room Artificer Baker, the 'Chief' of *Upholder*, was staggering along, steadying himself against the pitch and roll of the ship, and for a handhold he seized the jamb of the door. At that moment the heavy watertight door slammed shut trapping his fingers. The counter swing released them and Baker dropped to the deck, his fingers mangled.

A swift examination showed that three of his fingers were almost severed.

Even ashore such an injury was severe. On a submarine without even a sick berth steward, let alone a doctor, it was something to daunt the most courageous.

Wanklyn ransacked the glorified first-aid chest, with its strictly limited supplies and tackled the injury. Pause for a moment and visualise the scene.

The submarine was a tightly closed box of shining steel and a conglomerate of stinks, bad air, oil and fumes.

Wanklyn would have been completely justified in using a scalpel and amputating the smashed fingers.

Instead, with occasional reference to the book of instructions accompanying the medical chest he gave the necessary injections, delicately trimmed the mangled flesh, bound up the fingers and eased Baker's excruciating agony.

The ship was still four or five days away from Gibraltar with plenty of time for complications to arise following the injury but Wanklyn gave the smashed hand every attention.

On arrival Baker was sent to hospital and Lieutenant Crawford, meeting him on a later date was shown the hand by C.E.R.A. Baker. Apart from a malformation of one finger his hand was near normal

After a brief stay at Gibraltar *Upholder* was onward routed to Malta, a sea passage alive with menace. In fact, apart from submarines that route was virtually closed to sea traffic.

Once at Malta, having reported to Captain (S), *Upholder* joined the other submarines in Lazaretto Creek. After her tempestuous trip from

England, and the inevitable defects of a new ship, *Upholder* had to spend a little time under repairs.

Wanklyn used that, as did his crew for that matter, in getting themselves 'put into the picture' by the officers and crews of submarines already in service there.

They heard, for instance, that submarine *Triton* had raided the Italian coast, shelling towns from very close range. (*Triton's* gunner held an audience spellbound as he related that the flash from his gun had scorched washing hanging on a clothes-line ashore!) They heard, too, of *Truant* venturing so close to the Isle of Capri that they could hear Gracie Fields' soaring top notes coming to them over the sea and had contemplated asking her, over the Tannoy loud hailer to give that deathless favourite 'Sally', but refrained because it might give away their proximity to the coast.

A little tall yarning does nobody any harm over the daily tot.

But they heard, too, of the grimmer side. Of submarines which had failed to return, of boats attacking shipping which was pouring across to North Africa where Wavell's army was battling desperately, with its thin line of 'thirty thousand', to hold against Rommel, what they had gained from the Italians.

Meanwhile Wanklyn had been absorbing, from more constructive talks with commanding officers, details of the difficulties he would have to face, of the strong escorts which guarded the heavily loaded convoys, of the vicious and prolonged counter-attacks by surface ships.

He learned, too, that torpedoes were in short supply in Malta, the besieged island. Every one had to show a dividend. Ships in ballast were to be secondary targets. The primary objective would be a deeply laden troopship or supply transport forging ahead for North Africa.

The submarine force available could not hope to completely stop Rommel's supply convoys. All they could hope to do was to slow them down, sink some and force others to wait until a strong escort was available.

With the convoys attacked, some ships destroyed or damaged, and the others scattered it would prevent Rommel from mounting quite as strong an offensive as he would have liked, and would give Wavell time to turn his fingertip hold on Libya into a firm grip.

It was a momentous task, part of which *Upholder* was preparing to share.

Only stupid fools, utterly stupid fools pretend that imminent action is something they are waiting for, something they are longing to get 'stuck into'. And there were few, if any fools in the Malta submarines.

But for *Upholder's* crew the waiting for The Day was nearly as bad as actual action.

Finally it came: 24 January 1941

No blaring of trumpets, no emotional scenes, just a few brief good luck wishes and she slipped out of harbour small, self-contained, and just a little bit lonely if the truth be told.

She had been tried in the balance and found not wanting. Her crew had trained and trained until obedience to an order, instant obedience was now a matter of sheer reflex action.

The supreme test was all that remained.

To tackle the enemy.

Upholder cleared the harbour boom, trudged along the swept channel and at 2029 made her first dive. It was not a hurried dive but a trim dive by which all her qualities could be exquisitely adjusted. The stores, including the eight torpedoes had naturally altered her trim.

Wanklyn shut the conning-tower hatch and clipped it securely, at the same moment ordering: 'Open main vents.' His shabby uniform jacket seemed a little more oil-stained and disreputable than when *Upholder* had sailed from Portsmouth. His piratical beard was a little longer: his face was set in more determined lines.

Upholder's hydroplanes and motors forced her below the surface, and sleek sea covered the casing, swirled around the gun, covered the conning tower; and behold, the sea surface was deserted, showing hardly a ripple on its glassiness. But very shortly that surface was once more troubled by the ship's emergence. Thanks to skill and forethought little trimming was necessary: indeed, so perfect were her adjustments that she surfaced at 2037 – eight minutes to trim a submarine was almost phenomenal.

At 12 knots she proceeded on her lawful occasions, heading for the area allotted to her for the immediate operations.

'Its all yours,' said Wanklyn to the Officer of the Watch and went below to open his secret orders. He rubbed his large sensitive hands when he read that his immediate billet was in the vicinity of Tripoli – where most of the sea's excitements were liable to happen. Ashore in North Africa the fate of the civilised world hung in the balance: in most of the rest of Europe a state of stagnation appeared to have arisen.

The Tripoli coast promised a harvest. How difficult to garner that harvest would depend on the man in command. For twelve years he had trained rigorously for just this trip.

For nearly twelve months dockyard workmen had laboured to produce this ship, this slim, venomous tiger shark of a ship.

Now man and ship were joined.

What would the union produce?

CHAPTER 3

BLOODED

AT 0030 on the morning of Sunday, 26 January the look-out on *Upholder's* small bridge sighted Kerkenah Number 4 buoy. Wanklyn was able to confirm his position.

He was on offensive patrol.

In less than an hour the asdic rating reported: 'H.E. (hydrophone effect from moving propellers) bearing 090 degrees.'

Up on the bridge the blackness of the night enveloped the submarine like a dark blanket.

Look-outs and officers peered into the night.

They saw nothing. But Wanklyn closed in on the bearing given by the pinging asdic. He ordered 'diving stations'. Every order was reported three times to avoid risk of error. This was it. This was no exercise with a friendly surface ship, this was no routine dive on voyage. This was action.

Every man slipped swiftly to his appointed place. The engine-room ratings attended their engines, the asdic rating concentrated almost painfully on his pinging set, torpedo ratings carried out their duties in the torpedo-room. In the control-room the appointed men stood by the hydrophones, the asdic expert listened, the helmsman steered alertly, ears strained for each command; all hands were keyed up like harpstrings strained nearly to stiapping-point.

As yet the *Upholder* held to the surface: still nothing was visible. From the darkened bridge, where no betraying glimmer of light showed, Wanklyn ordered: 'Stand by one and two torpedoes!' If anything, the atmosphere of tense strain grew tauter, every man was keyed up to that pitch which enables action to follow thought in the fraction of a second.

At 0130 the asdic rating grunted: 'H.E. moving left.' The officer near at hand in the control-room yelled into the 'pig's ear' of the voice-pipe: 'Bridge-H. E. moving left.' Wanklyn altered course and even as he did so he sighted one shadowy merchant ship escorted by one destroyer. The enemy was in view, practically at his mercy. And Hitler had declared Total War – no mercy for the vanquished. Wanklyn repeated his order: 'Standby one and two torpedoes!' The most difficult attack of all was about to take place – an attack on the surface. His emotionless voice rapped out 'Fire one!' A few seconds later the voice-pipe carried the message 'Fire two!'

Upholder shuddered twice momentarily as the torpedoes left the tubes and whined on their way toward the target – the merchant ship – a more valuable prize for the moment than an elusive destroyer.

At 0131 Wanklyn altered course to avoid the escort, and at that moment sighted two more ships following in open order. A ragged convoy indeed.

'Stand by three and four torpedoes!'

Minutes had elapsed from the firing of one and two torpedoes without the resulting 'crump' that signalled a hit.

Thirteen minutes after making his first attack Wanklyn snapped, 'Fire three, fire four.'

Again Upholder shuddered. 'Dive, Dive, Dive.'

Upholder slid beneath the surface. Everybody listened intently. There was no under-water explosion.

In her first attack she had fired four torpedoes at two ships. And all had missed.

Nobody spoke, men just glanced at one another, and went on with their jobs. Wanklyn, upon whom the success of this first attack had rested showed no emotion beyond a thoughtful stroking of his beard.

At 0240, half an hour later he ordered: 'Surface, Blow main ballast.'

The routine must go on, batteries required charging in readiness for the long daylight dives.

At dawn she dived for the day and during that submerged day Wanklyn went over and over the recent attack, move by move, seeking a reason for failure. There had been no counter-attack by the escorts, no deluge of heart-shaking depth-charges, no obvious violent change of course by the transports.

He had missed. And the merchant ships had gone on their way, unscathed, if not serenely.

The next night, on the surface, she sighted three merchant ships, closed for attack, but broke it off. They were sailing light, that is unloaded.

It must have been a temptation to resist, to try just one torpedo on a ship.

Early next morning, shortly after three o'clock, *Upholder* closed in to attack what seemed to be a promisingly large target. Two tubes were at the stand-by the crew tensed and ready.

Then the bridge personnel recognised the target. It was a villa ashore. So close inshore was *Upholder* that in the darkness the house, looming vaguely and whitely, resembled the bridge of a ship.

Forty-five minutes later the first streaks of false dawn began to lighten the sky. Soon she would have to dive again, but there would be the chance for a last look-see around in the Indian hour when surface ships loom large and a submarine still remains inconspicuous.

And something loomed.

Two large ships, one of them an armed merchant cruiser and the other an 8,000-ton motor vessel.

Wanklyn closed in.

At 0427 came 'Fire one, Fire two.'

One minute later a solid thump came through the water.

'A hit.'

A mixture of a growl of satisfaction and a brief cheer rang through her as Wanklyn ordered: 'Dive.'

Upholder had been blooded.

The armed merchant cruiser was not equipped to fight under-water craft. She carried no detecting devices at all, but she could let out a heart-rending, soulful yelp for help, so Wanklyn cautiously circled his victim and waited a little more than two hours before he lifted the periscope barely above surface.

He had aimed well. The stricken ship was stopped, her bows were already under water almost to the bridge. Wanklyn said: 'She won't need any further attention. She'll sink all right.' And altered course for the western end of his patrol area.

She was submerged in the afternoon of 30 January when the asdic rating reported: 'Convoy approaching from the west.'

Wanklyn caught the periscope as it climbed from its housing. From his knees to full height he rose with it. As the frothing water drained from the uppermost glass he saw the convoy escort, a destroyer and another ship, which he estimated at 5,000 tons.

'Down periscope, Group up.... . Forty feet.' The rapped orders followed one another smoothly and were as smoothly obeyed. The grouped-up motors pushed her along at 9 knots.

'Stand by three and four tubes.' Then 'Group down, slow ahead, periscope depth, up periscope.'

Wanklyn was ready to attack.

'Fire three.' A second's pause. 'Fire four.'

Upholder shuddered as the torpedoes left the tubes. 'Down periscope. Eighty feet. Silent routine.' Even the clang of a dropped spanner would be picked up by the escort. In his swift glance around before diving Wanklyn had seen a destroyer racing at full speed for him.

They heard a 'crump' but almost instantly it was merged in a savage volcanic eruption. The deck under-foot shook and shuddered, the lights above were smashed into tinkling splinters, the ballast pumps on their rubber beds shook like jellies. The din punished the eardrums.

Upholder was living through her first depth-charge attack. The destroyer turned on her heel for another attack, and yet another. Wanklyn started his game of hide and seek. When the destroyer stopped he stopped. When it moved he moved on a new course. A deeper dive, for full sneed ahead. It was for all the world like a hare doubling and twisting in a race for the Waterloo Cup. Another vicious pattern of depth-charges was like the snap of a pursuing greyhound's teeth. The ominous silence was shattered. More lights crashed and tinkled down. Like a captured hare in a greyhound's jaws *Upholder* shook and writhed.

'Stop both!' ordered Wanklyn the imperturbable, as the asdic expert reported the destroyer stopped dead. Then, hard on the heels of that announcement: 'Destroyer coming in again,' he stated.

'Group up!' Wanklyn countered.

Throughout her length *Upholder* shuddered and squirmed as her screws pushed her away from that deadly danger-zone. In fifteen minutes twenty-five depth-charges had rained down around her. She made her getaway slickly, and the watchkeeper logged: 'Probably a 5,000-tonner!' Nothing more – no vainglorious claims. The submarine set course for Malta. Her first patrol ended on 1 February 1941. As she tied up alongside submarine *Triumph* in Malta Harbour, an air-raid crashed a resounding welcome.

The net result of this first foray was one 8,000-ton motor vessel sunk without doubt; one 5,000-tonner a probable, with the accent on something more than probable.

Who can blame the crew of *Upholder* if they strutted a little on their return to Base. There was much to celebrate and little with which to celebrate it.

Even in the early days of 1941, before the position became acute, food was ominously short for all.

Beer remained but a memory. It was almost unprocurable. Some of the crew, determined to celebrate somehow had sampled the noxious brew ambeet: a vinegary concoction more popularly known as 'boiled oil' or 'Stuka juice'. The latter was nearer the accurate description in view of its explosive qualities. This chained lightning hit a man with all the stunning impact of a bomb.

But, it is a poor heart which never rejoices and *Upholder's* crew had something about which to rejoice. They had been blooded on their first trip. They had paid a dividend in their first balance sheet.

On a more serious note, and one which disturbed them, all, both officers and men, was the lack of mail. What little of it trickled through was weeks and weeks old, most of it tragically lay at the bottom of the Mediterranean.

Men did not know how their families were faring in sorely tried England, and had no means of knowing whether their letters were arriving home.

Actually David Wanklyn received no letters for three months although Elspeth wrote three and four times a week. And worried secretly because there was no mail from him.

In the meantime *Upholder* had to be prepared, in between vicious air raids, for another patrol. Eventually came the day: 12 February. At eleven o'clock in the morning they moved off from the Base in Lazaretto Creek, their 'steaming-bags' over their shoulders. Sartorially they were something to marvel at. Some wore off-white long sweaters, a favourite in submarines, while others contented themselves with more prosaic overalls. Anything less like a group of hard-bitten fighting men was hard to imagine. In only one point was there unanimity.

On their hats they had the tally ribbons tied in 'tiddley bows' a small coin trapped in the bow.

A few 'good lucks' deeply, fervently, floated after them.

That was all.

Last aboard was Wanklyn walking with long, easy strides, his shabby uniform jacket just a bit more disreputable than before his first trip from Malta. Beneath it he, too, wore a sweater. His cap was oil- and grease-stained.

The floating catwalk swayed as he strode over it. He climbed the steel rungs of the conning tower with easy familiarity and swung his legs over.

'All ready for sea, Sir.' Lieutenant Crawford greeted him.

'Thank you, Number One.' Then, 'Let go for'ard. Let go aft. Slow ahead, port.'

Upholder was once more on the move. She slipped through the boom defence, met her local escort which would guide her through the swept channels. The yellow sand rock of Malta dropped astern.

For a couple of hours *Upholder* exercised with her escort carrying out dummy attacks at periscope depth, for Wanklyn never missed an opportunity to improve technique.

Then farewells, a wave from the bearded figure on her bridge and the two ships parted company, the escort to return to battered Malta, *Upholder* once more to patrol off the coast of Tripoli.

It was a familiar and relaxed scene inside the submarine. On the table were the charts of the Tripoli coast. The Engine Room Artificer was closed up on the diving panel, the helmsman at the wheel, and a couple of off-watch ratings at the foot of the ladder inhaling the nearest approach to fresh air they would get for a while. The 'gash' – rubbish and scraps from the last meal, was in buckets waiting for the order from the bridge for it to be dumped at darkness. Too much attention could not be paid to that seemingly simple operation. More than one submarine had been traced through an unpunctured cigarette-tin being thrown carelessly overboard.

A trail of galley and mess-deck debris winding over a millpond sea has been known to give away a ship's probable course.

Although still literally on her own doorstep *Upholder* slipped into a routine which on a submarine is a mixture of alertness and relaxed continuation of a normal job.

'She's all yours,' Wanklyn said to the Officer of the Watch and slipped below. Down to the familiar mixture of submarine smells of packed humanity, stale smell of food, oil and thrice-breathed air.

Automatically he glanced at the clock: 1915. He placed his night glasses where he could grab them without wasting a second and sat down.

At that moment a rating bawled: 'Captain on the bridge.' To any submarine commanding officer that cry means, 'Get up topsides as quick as all hell. Something is brewing.'

Wanklyn shot through the control-room and shinned up the conning tower trunking as quickly as ever he had shinned up a tree in boyhood days.

'Object ahead. Can't make it out,' the Officer of the Watch reported.

Wanklyn studied the vague shadow ahead. Delicately he adjusted his glasses. The shadow still refused to reveal any more identity.

'Can you make anything of it, sir?' the Officer of the Watch asked.

'Call diving stations,' Wanklyn snapped.

It was too low in the water to be a freighter. 'E-boat, possibly,' Wanklyn guessed.

Below him the boat was ready. The fore end, the business department was manned, engine-room and motor-room quickened into movement like an anthill casually trodden on.

This was only a few hours out, and only a few miles from Malta.

Upholder was about to deal with a client on her own doorstep.

At that moment the sky behind them blazed into a cone of white light.

'Searchlights over Malta, Sir,' came from the after look-out. Despite the intently peering eyes staring ahead which he longed to join, his job was to report ANYTHING astern, and searchlights were something astern.

In the diffused glow the object ahead became slightly clearer. Slowly *Upholder* forged ahead toward it the placid water gurgling around her casing.

Without moving his glasses from his eyes Wanklyn spoke.

'It's a U-boat!'

CHAPTER 4

MYSTERIOUS SUBMARINE

'A U-BOAT!'

A killer and it was about to be killed. Dog eat dog. A target worth a full salvo of four torpedoes. Sinking her would mean not only one enemy less, but would be the saving of many ships which she might have sunk in the future.

'A U-boat!'

It was whispered throughout the length of the British submarine. The effect was electric. Thumbs up! The Torpedo Gunner's Mate caressed the firing lever. These torpedoes would have to run true if he followed them down the tube and had to steer them.

Upholder crept in relentlessly.

Wanklyn knew that this was a happy hunting ground for U-boats, the few surface ships making for Malta, as well as warships, could wriggle and twist as much as they liked in the open water, ultimately they would have to come to Malta and there the U-boats waited.

From the situation report he knew that no British submarine would be in the vicinity.

Two thousand yards, 1,500 yards. *Upholder* was in a perfect position for an attack. Any second now would come the order 'Fire!' and the U-boat would be a shambles dropping to the depths with only a slimy oil patch on the surface to show where she had been.

The atmosphere inside the submarine became electric. 'Why doesn't the Old Man fire 'em? What's he trying to do? Go alongside the damn U-boat?'

The older hands counselled patience. This was going to be no near-miss.

At the back of everybody's mind was the lurking thought that quite possibly the U-boat was doing a bit of stalking on her own account. Keen eyes on her bridge might have spotted *Upholder*. At this moment a man's hand might be resting on the firing lever on her, ready to send four torpedoes snaking through the dark waters at *Upholder*.

Suddenly Wanklyn spoke.

'Signalman, make a challenge to that vessel.'

A challenge? A flashing light which would give away *Upholder's* position? There were no British submarines in that area. And any others would be enemies.

The signalman lifted his Aldis lamp to his eye.

'That looks like a T-class sub.' Wanklyn said levelly. A T-class sub., a British sub. where one should not be. Where one COULD not be if the situation report was correct.

The signalman clicked the trigger and the light flickered across the dark waters making the challenge, the letter for the night.

No reply.

If it was a U-boat and she was stalking *Upholder* then the British submarine had given her a wonderful pin-pointed target.

Upholder crept in.

'Challenge again.'

The light flickered once more.

No reply.

'And again.'

For the third time the Aldis lamp sent its staccato query over the water, the sound of the lamp's trigger sounding like thunder-claps to those on the bridge of *Upholder*.

Was the U-boat planning a surface action? Had her gunlayer got the dark bulk of the British ship framed in his sights?

Wanklyn finally broke the tension:

'That's a T-class submarine. Break off the attack, resume zigzag course.'

The eyes which had trained with infinite patience at bird-watching had detected, even in the darkness, the comparatively trifling differences between a U-boat and one which sailed under the White Ensign.

Now, after one challenge had been ignored Wanklyn would have been completely justified in sinking the target. According to the situation report, which gave the approximate position of our subs. there should not have been one in that vicinity. In fact not within many miles.

I was on that submarine, that T-class sub. that night. I was on watch in the engine-room at the time *Upholder* was stalking her. I have never since failed to be extremely thankful, and grateful for Wanklyn's keen eyesight. After all, in his complete bag of enemy shipping he included three U-boats. The chances of a submarine escaping unscathed from such an attack as he mounted that night would have been infinitesimal.

We were returning from a long and punishing patrol. Malta was only a couple of hours away. We had fired fifteen torpedoes and the last remaining one was jammed in the tube. We had also been damaged when one of our torpedoes had hit and set off a mine uncomfortably close.

We had also been in a surface gun battle. The crew to a man was weary. Ten hours or so more would see its relaxing in Lazaretto Creek – so far as the air raids allowed men to relax.

Normal routine was being followed. The stokers in the engine-room were whistling softly in harmony. A couple of ratings were enjoying the luxury of a smoke in the control-room. Somewhere a game of cards, with vocal accompaniment was going on.

We were returning from patrol before time and because of damage had no means of reporting that we were doing so and would be in that vicinity at that time.

Even after this long lapse of time a discreet veil had better be drawn over the reasons, or excuses, for the failure on the part of an Officer of the Watch and two look-outs failing to see not only one challenge but three.

Possibly they were temporarily viewing the background of weaving searchlights, anti-aircraft bursts and listening to the dull crump of bombs around the harbour which would soon be theirs. Viewing it with mixed feelings.

Maybe.

Upholder continued on her course and eventually reached her patrol area on 18 February around noon. For a while she lay submerged to periscope depth watching the little water boats entering that arid water. Later, during the half darkness, she saw three merchant ships and moved to attack. But they were so close inshore, and merged with the background that it was impossible to get a clear-cut silhouette of them. To have chanced a torpedo would have meant risking a miss with the torpedo going off among the rocks thus informing all and sundry that a British sub. was in the area.

Upholder allowed them to pass. There would be another day.

That evening, while on the surface, they picked up three merchant ships escorted by three destroyers.

With an escort that size the ships were obviously of some importance.

Upholder went into her usual slick attacking routine. Wanklyn took her in to 2,000 yards, then 1,500 yards. He passed down the side of one of the destroyers at less than 1,000 yards.

Once his torpedoes hit he could expect a depth-charge attack of no mean magnitude.

The leading merchant ship was nicely placed for blowing out of the water.

'Fire one. Fire two.'

Upholder then dived to 180 feet, but there were no satisfying explosions.

They had missed.

Throughout the patrol the weather had been foul – foul that is for submarines. The sea remained like a sheet of blue-green glass. Even in the early morning and late evening only the most obtuse of look-outs could have failed to spot the 'feather' when *Upholder* put up her periscope.

So Wanklyn returned to Malta and entered Grand Harbour on 23 February. He described his patrol as 'uneventful'. Uneventful it might have been by orthodox veiwing but for this submarine to return without being able to claim at least one sinking was unusual

Upholder's crew by this time had assessed the qualities – and failings – of night life in Malta. Seldom a night passed without the island being heavily bombed and to the ratings ashore on liberty it seemed as if the Italian-German bombers seemed to be making a dead set at just the place they had chosen for their meagre evening's entertainment.

There was not much fun in going ashore for a night out and having to spend most of it in a crowded air-raid shelter, or scurrying back to the Base with fragments of anti-aircraft shells dropping about their ears.

Nobody pretended that they were eager for the next patrol, but while on it some of the phoney shore life could be relegated to the backgrounds of their minds. For the time being their little world was encased in that 630 tons of steel,

They knew, too, that the happy return of a submarine was a chancy thing, as even money a bet as flipping a coin. But, on the other hand, they stood a reasonable chance of hitting back.

Once on patrol, life became a matter of routine. A game of ludo (a popular game with submariners as much for the arguments it could produce as for the merits of the game) would be under way in the Ratings' Mess for'ard. In the Petty Officers' Mess a complicated and important game of cribbage was being pursued.

Beyond the low-voiced comments, the click of the dice and lighter click as a counter was placed in position, or the subdued 'fifteen two, fifteen four, an' three's seven', as a P.O. explored his meagre 'box', there was little sound.

The hum of the motors was an *obbligato*.

As for the rest of the crew off watch, they were luxuriating in their favourite recreation – sleep.

So *Upholder* slipped along on her next patrol. Wanklyn lay on his narrow bunk confident that the Officer of the Watch would see he was called immediately for anything worth while.

He listened to the hiss as the periscope slid up and down in its oil-bath, subconsciously assayed the multitude of other minor sounds which assured him that his submarine was running as she should.

And he was called.

'Two ships up top, sir.' Wanklyn looked at the depth-gauge. Twenty-eight feet.

'Up periscope.'

Wanklyn met it on his knees and rose with it. Somebody passed him a sheet of tissue paper with which he wiped the moisture from the eyepiece.

His thumb checked the rating raising the periscope.

There were two ships. Two minelayers, but they were too far away for attack and increasing their distance. 'Down periscope.'

The targets vanished into the morning haze, the game of crib was resumed, the dice clicked and men went back to their sleep.

And *Upholder* slipped along through the underwater like a long lean shark.

Patrols had their moments of *ennui* as well as breath-taking tension.

CHAPTER 5

BOARDERS AWAY

Upholder was four days out on patrol on 25 April when, around 1400 she spotted a motor vessel. 'Diving stations.'

Wanklyn seemed to crouch with his eyes almost touching the deck as he met the rising periscope.

'Stand by one and two torpedoes.'

'He signalled for more height, checked the rise and swept through the whole 360 degrees before concentrating on the target. She might be bait for a trap, a lurking destroyer or motor boat, or even an aircraft could be in the offing.

The attack team gathered around Wanklyn, almost breathing down his neck. He arrayed all the factors to be taken into account, even in that tideless sea. Speed of target, speed of torpedo, angular deflection, casual local currents and their speed, some of them insignificant in themselves, but in the mass important and could mean difference between a hit and a target scurrying away distant waters, frightened out of her wits by a near miss.

Fifteen hundred yards … One thousand. His eyes were still glued to the eyepiece.

'Fire one. Fire two.'

Two soft 'pooshes' of air breathed through her. Wanklyn saw the tracks of his torpedoes running true. 'Down periscope.'

Lips set into tight lines as they waited.

Forty seconds … forty-five … fifty … then 'Crump !' A hit.

This was going to be no blank patrol.

Wanklyn stroked his beard slowly and reflectively. He looked around his attack team and they saw the glimmering of a smile crease his face.

An obvious supply ship for North Africa and they had hit her.

A couple of peeps through the periscope to make certain that she was gone were sufficient. Then *Upholder* moved from the vicinity.

It was her third kill, a 5,500-ton motor ship and loaded deep.

The next day *Upholder* closed in toward Kerkenah Bank, checked her position by the buoy so conveniently placed there. After a careful study around the 360 degrees Wanklyn ordered: 'Diving stations. Surface.' Then after a quick look round from the bridge 'Dive.'

Aerial reconnaissance had reported one merchant ship and one destroyer aground on that bank. Both were on an even keel, apparently little damaged and both capable of being salvaged.

Wanklyn had other ideas. His first intention was to donate a torpedo each to the sitting ducks. But there were snags. There might be a shallow patch between *Upholder* and the stranded ships which would divert his torpedoes, might even explode them.

For three or four hours he crept around working plot after plot, still keeping a wary eye open for any craft likely to be playing nursemaid to the two ships. Toward evening he closed in slowly on the merchant ship from the west where, against the setting sun he would be difficult to pick up, while he would have his target clearly outlined. By this time *Upholder's* crew could scarcely breathe with excitement. They knew that something out of the ordinary was brewing. This was no steady stalk, fire torpedoes and submerge deeply for the getaway. This was going to be something to rank with the raid on the *Altmark* in the distant Norwegian fjord.

Well! The Navy had been there. The Navy was here, too.

At 1940 Wanklyn moved in with periscope just peeping above the water, a couple of hundred yards more and the ship would be a shattered hulk. A duck sitting waiting for it.

With a shuddering corkscrew motion *Upholder* came to a dead stop.

She was aground! Hard on the bank like the two helpless ships less than a thousand yards away. Twenty-nine feet showed on the depth-gauge.

Just what he had suspected. A rib or ridge of bank lay between *Upholder* and the merchant ship and a whole shallow bank protected the destroyer.

Our aerial investigation had reported two ships ashore on the bank. Now, was some enemy plane to report also that a British submarine had joined the increasing population on Kerkenah Bank?

Wanklyn swiftly estimated the risks and decided to take them. So far as he could see the merchant ship was deserted. There was no sign of life on her. But there MIGHT be a gun-crew or two.

He blew his tanks and surfaced. Below him was the muddy treacherous bank but a few feet under his keel. Slowly he took her ahead. It was delicate, precise seamanship and ship handling. At any moment she could touch again and he had to be ready to put her full astern at the slightest touch. Six hundred and thirty tons of ship moving only slowly ahead can drive herself well and truly into a sandbank.

But there came no touch.

Then Wanklyn gave the order: 'Stand-by boarding party.'

This WAS going to rank with *Cossack* and the *Altmark*. The boarding party stood by as Wanklyn sidled *Upholder* close alongside the merchant ship. Only a narrowing ribbon of water lay between them. Every ear was strained for the sound of an aircraft as *Upholder* reduced the ribbon to nothing. It was 2030

All the party, bridge personnel and boarders could see in the moonlight the dark and looming bulk of her bridge, could see the name painted on her flank: *Arta*, just as they could discern the lorries, cars and motorcycles on her decks. Here was a fish worth catching, if ever; transport was a crying need for the Afrika Korps.

Lieutenant Christopher Read was in charge of the small, very select boarding party. They scrambled up the enemy's side in the good old fashion in obedience to the seldom heard call of 'Boarders awa-a-ay!'

Those who scrambled up the rusted side found an empty ship-empty of men, anyhow, though the munitions were plentiful enough. There was no opposition -not even a token resistance. Two of *Arta's* holds were fitted for the reception of German troops. Read and his boarders collected ample samples of the plentiful spoil left behind when the ship was abandoned. There were arms, flags, papers, helmets, and even a staff officer's picnic basket. It was not wholesale looting: merely proof of the effort they had made. They laid an explosive charge by the huge safe in the Captain's cabin.

The prize's holds were flooded 'tweendeck high in all compartments; that destroyed all chance of exploring the main cargo she bore. The boarding party thoroughly enjoyed their hour's stay aboard the *Arta*. Call them the privateers of 1941! It is seldom enough in modern war that such an opportunity offers: normally all that is left is a tortured horror of riven steel and charred woodwork.

During the boarding, one of the boarding party, A.B. Saunders, spotted a pair of boots; they seemed about his size. He decided they were a prize worth having and in the darkness grabbed the boots but dropped them smartly when he found a dead German still in them!

After some sixty minutes of exploration, Read and his men had done all within their power, and they returned to their submarine. At 2144 the explosive charges went off most effectively, setting fire to the *Arta*. Duty completed, *Upholder* groped her way steadily clear of the Kerkenah; and her interested crew watched the fire resulting in explosions spreading with satisfactory rapidity. The motor-cycles and the big trucks crowding the upper decks made the prettiest blaze they had ever seen, most of them declared.

Flames reached high into the surprised sky. The entire Kerkenah Bank glowed like a pagan celebration party.

At dawn of Sunday, the 27th, the submarine dived and cruised around at periscope depth till evening. The illuminations had not attracted any enemy activity. There was no great depth of water around the Bank in which a submarine could play about it; but there was a lot to be learned in the art of shoal-water navigation, in view of the future. Wanklyn like any other perfectionist, believed in learning lessons at first hand. His submarine was a valuable fighting tool, not to be risked unnecessarily; so the more he knew of the waters of her operation the better the prospect of sensational results.

In the main that Sunday was peaceful and placid; until 1930 showed on the clock. It was almost time to surface when the semi-somnolent crew received a rude awakening: their vessel shuddered and quivered so that even the rivets rattled; the telegraphs in the motor-room rang to 'Stop!' At periscope depth she had bottomed obviously the shoal-water charts had not fully explained the difficulties. She stayed there until 2000 until her Commander called hands to diving stations. Never was a call more welcome; inside the cramped hull the air was growing thick and clammy, free, fresh air would be a godsend even if the relieved lungs would be instantly filled with cigarette smoke.

'Blow main ballast!' was the order. A flurry of bubbles broke the calm sea's surface; Upholder emerged among the frothing turmoil.

'Stop blowing!'

Wanklyn unclipped the conning-tower hatch, the air pressure from within flung it open. He was on the bridge in a flash: the look-outs sprang smartly to their bridge positions.

'Half ahead, both motors!' The engines started sucking welcome air into *Upholder's* interior. All was well with the submarine world – or was it?

Forty minutes later the look-outs were flung against the conning-tower cowl. Down below the question on all lips was: 'What the hell's happening now!' The submarine was shuddering convulsively. The telegraphs rang 'Full speed astern!' The boat had bottomed once more, this time in a scant 15 feet of water. High time these shoal waters were re-surveyed. *Upholder* bucked, plunged and thrashed like a harpooned whale – the simile is very apt – until the drag of her reversed screws brought her off into deeper water, clear of that treacherous muddy bottom. Had an enemy aircraft shown up at that juncture, H.M. submarine must have been written off as a total loss.

On 1 May her periscope occasionally broke surface; beneath that wary eye the silent mole-like shape glided stealthily through the water, that here was crystal clear to an overhead observer, had there been such. For the deeper areas of the Mediterranean are like the finest glass, concealing nothing, unlike our opaque northern waters. Only the control-room orders broke the internal hush. And then, at 1102, as the water drained off the periscope glass, Wanklyn spotted what he was in search of – an enemy convoy.

'Diving stations! Down periscope ... Group up!' Almost whispered orders. 'Full ahead!' The boat was alive and astir in a breath; lights flickered on in all compartments. The vessel quivered as she gathered speed. Some submarines are like that, as if their material construction throbbed with the same life and hopes of their human complements. With sweet precision the attack team surrounded Wanklyn.

Lieutenant Crawford watched the ratings controlling the hydroplanes and instantly rectified any slight alteration in the *Upholder's* trim.

'Group down. Slow ahead. Up periscope.' The tall double-jointed figure of David Wanklyn was in tune to the last nerve and muscle. He caught the handles with ease as the instrument zizzed up from the well. He came up slowly from a crouch. The stoker controlling the periscope watched like a hawk for any sign from his Commander that the instrument was high enough. Up went Wanklyn's thumb; and the upward climb was arrested.

The chief hunter of this submerged *shikari* scanned the sky, swept the sea all round, and then concentrated on the convoy. He counted aloud: an incredible tally: 'One, two, three, four, five' – then a brief pause; followed: 'Six, seven, eight, nine!' What a convoy! Almost as if in awe at his unbelievable luck, he said: 'Down periscope. Stand by one, two, three and four tubes!' His eyes glinted. He stroked his beard. 'There are five supply ships and four destroyers up there!' he reported, and as an afterthought: 'They must be extremely valuable to have such an escort!'

'Up periscope!' As the invaluable instrument burst through the thin skin of water he could see two destroyers ahead of the convoy and two others on starboard beam and quarter. It was 1145. Silence reigned in the control-room; a silence that only the unhurried breathing of its occupants broke. With his eyes glued to the periscope, Wanklyn said in a hushed voice: 'Fire one!' The boat bumped. 'Fire two!' Another shudder. 'Fire three – fire four!' At that critical moment he undoubtedly wished he had double the number of tubes at his disposal. Here was manna from Heaven if ever.

'All torpedoes running!' reported the asdic rating; like a quick echo 'Down periscope!' left Wanklyn's lip. Wanklyn could do no more: the issue was in the hands of the sea-gods. He could merely wait and listen and breathe a silent prayer for success and survival, for convoy and escort were zigzagging energetically.

Three dull explosions disturbed that awed silence below as two torpedoes ripped the side of the 6,000-ton German Fels liner, and a third tore open the chilled steel plating of a 7,386-ton motor vessel.

'Up periscope!' Wanklyn's keen eyes glinted at what they saw: the Fels liner was sinking rapidly by the stern, the motor vessel was listing heavily, and stopped. Three other supply ships and as many destroyers were streaking away as if the devil himself were scorching their tails. The remaining destroyer skirmished around at large, dropping depth-charges which rumbled and crashed and destroyed all the previous calm.

'Down periscope! Sixty feet – and now, how about a cup of tea?' That cool nonchalance was so typical of the man that grins broke the set faces of those near by.

Forward, the appointed ratings worked like demons re-loading the tubes – only two torpedoes remained, alas! The haphazard depth-charging created no real trouble for *Upholder*, for at 1900 the submarine had closed in to within 1,200 yards of the damaged ship. A swift glance through his periscope showed to Wanklyn that the stricken victim, though heavily listed, was still on an even fore-and-aft keel.

'Stand by one and two tubes!' He noted the destroyer still close by, but the supply ship was by far the most valuable target. 'Fire one. Fire two!' Twice the *Upholder* shuddered characteristically: a quiver like that of an alert terrier scenting a kill. The air pressure within increased. Almost as this fact became noticeable, two heavy explosions shook the British submarine like kicks from a giant foot.

Two hits – certain! Fifteen minutes later *Upholder* shook and writhed to the force of three additional explosions. Calmly enough Wanklyn observed: 'Maybe depth-charges; as likely to be boiler explosions!'

Upholder's magic eye was raised again. At 1940 Wanklyn observed the stern of the motor vessel just visible above the water, with the destroyer standing bewilderedly by. Another fifteen minutes and the stricken prey plunged deep. Wanklyn stood calmly back, as calmly ordered: 'Down periscope!' and then, almost as casually as he had spoken throughout the engagement: 'Head for home!'

On 3 May *Upholder* entered Lazaretto Creek. Her Jolly Roger flew high and defiantly, in token of her successful patrol: a fitting homecoming for the little band of dedicated men of the under-water breed.

After tying up in the Creek, who could resist displaying those German helmets and flags: spoil from the destroyed *Arta*. Certainly not the triumphant men of the *Upholder*. Observers saw them on the sub.'s casing, crowned with their plundered helmets, waving the captured bunting. The *dghaisa* men watched in amazement from their gondola-like boats. A rumour flew round the harbour like wildfire that a German U-boat had arrived in the guarded harbour to surrender personally to Captain 'Shrimp' Simpson: Captain Submarines, 10th Flotilla!

The last entry in *Upholder's* log for her sixth patrol read: 'Hands paid. Make and mend'. The crew of the valiant craft were accorded a half-day's holiday in order to spend their pay and receive the praise of envious fellow-submariners.

On 5 May *Upholder* slipped her moorings and proceeded to the torpedo depot.

During the morning she had a 'hot run' in Number three tube. The torpedo motor started on its own accord. Tragically this resulted in the death of Petty Officer Carter and serious injury to Lieutenant Read who had led the raid on the Italian ship *Arta*.

To have lived through so much in the past few days and to emerge unscathed only to meet fate in friendly waters from one of her own faulty torpedoes was ironic enough.

CHAPTER 6

BY GUESS AND BY GOD

MANY people have asked, and will continue to ask 'How did these submariners, who lived an unnatural life in conditions almost unimaginable by the uninitiated, spend their scanty leisure on that war-torn, near shattered island of Malta, where everything except deadly danger appeared to be in short supply?' Beer and food were especially scarce, and the normal occupants of Malta were growing gaunter and more shaken every day. Even so, these men contrived to find enjoyment, as is the habit of the Navy when on shore, for after a patrol chockful of risks and hair-raising escapades, even the mildest form of pleasure can become almost an orgy.

Meeting them in the wrecked streets, you could hardly distinguish the breed from any other group of naval ratings, but, looking a little more closely, you would notice they carried themselves a little more cockily than the general service men; too, that their complexions were a little sallower, more pasty from lack of fresh air and sunshine; and if such characteristics didn't adequately identify them, the legend H.M. SUBMARINES, shining in gold from their cap-ribbons would dispel the last doubts.

You would encounter them along the Sliema sea-front, and in the plentiful bars and saloons of that area, as merry as sandboys and, quite often, afflicted, to put it mildly, with a slight alcoholic excess. And why not? Liquor could be got even if it were only indifferent ambeet. One or two other sources of supply are still on the secret list. There may one day be another war!

Submariners always clung together when ashore, like the two-legged wolf-packs they were. In one-for-all-and-all-for-one groups they sang their own special submarine songs, such as:

> Come to the spare crew; two bob a day,
> Come to the spare crew now.
> Joyful, joyful we will always be,
> When the boats have all gone out to sea,
> Sweeping up the mess-decks; nothing else to do;
> Come to the spare crew now ... etc.

This ditty was a challenge: a skit aimed at men who were held as spare crews for submarines; a challenge that they wouldn't be happy anywhere else other than in their own special under-water craft.

Or perhaps you would hear them bawling a song which went:

> If ever you're in trouble, Jack, for God's sake don't come home:
> You've been a nuisance all your life! ... and so on.

There was none of the heel-clicking, Heil Hitler stuff about these men. They either came back triumphant, or they – didn't, and the silent seas wrapped their fate in mystery. Theirs was a serial fight: all or nothing; they knew it, and preferred to take it fighting, when 'it' came. Such were the types of men whom David Wanklyn had under his command: specialists in death and destruction. In them Wanklyn had to have implicit confidence, just as they had in him, in whose judgment at sea they must wholly and solely rely.

And what about Wanklyn's own so-called leisure ashore in the unsafe safety of Malta? First and foremost he liked a well-won sleep: since, in *Upholder*, he slept like an old-time Indian scout: 'With both eyes open and his rifle by his side' – his subconscious ever on the alert for the unexpected, tensed for that instant action in a way which characterises the attitude of all great leaders of men when crisis is imminent. Occasionally he indulged in a little run ashore with friends of a similar kidney, and the bar of the Officers' Mess was not unknown to him. He could join in rollicking wardroom fun with the best of them and soon become the life and soul of any party with which he foregathered. His favourite party-piece was 'Contortionist', a turn that always aroused much enthusiasm among his audiences. To enact the role he, being double-jointed, would place his feet neatly behind his neck and appear as a legless wonder. His mother has remarked that it was horrible to see him do this: her attitude being the motherly one of 'Suppose you were struck like that!' but his fellow merrymakers found it enjoyable enough: probably because, when not so engaged, Wanklyn's general pose was one of concentrated seriousness.

But the times in which he found most satisfying enjoyment were those he spent in planning and scheming future attacks, strategy and deadly tactics with his close friend and senior: Captain 'Shrimp' Simpson.

Neither commanding officer, junior officers nor ratings during, this spell of liberty knew that the imminent patrol would bring the highest honour of all to their relaxed C.O. Never a man of them had a vague idea of what the future held for *Upholder*, as on 15 May she turned her stern to the joys and sorrows of Malta and faced the mystery of open waters again. But, as usual, every man dreamed of fresh victories, since triumphant returns bred a feeling of high elation. And the need for victories was urgently increasing as the situation in North Africa deteriorated so alarmingly.

At five minutes to nine next morning a convoy was sighted through *Upholder's* periscope, and hopes ran high in the control-room, but after a twenty-minute under-water chase, Wanklyn broke off his meditated attack, as the convoy was out of range, and torpedoes were too precious to be wasted on vague shots into the blue.

Four days of diving by day, surfacing by night went by; four days of pure boredom to these 'toilers' as the submarine loitered off the Sicilian coast, eager as a tiger on the prowl.

At 1800 on 20 May *Upholder* was cruising just beneath the surface, her crew waiting for the order 'Diving stations!' which was expected momentarily, as the need to sweeten the foul air inside was growing urgent. They were aware of the speed-up of their over-exerted hearts if any physical exertion was called for, that being the effect of the vitiated atmosphere. Oh, yes, that air was foul enough all right, and no error. One wag of the lower deck suggested that one-half the complement should breathe in whilst the other half breathed out – to give everyone a chance. Not until 1832, however, did the order come: 'Diving stations!'

It was the call to action, not to the surface. As the inevitable tension grew throughout the submarine's length, Wanklyn peered grimly, steadily through the periscope. Then a succession of orders and items of information came from his compressed lips:

'Down periscope. Group up. Full ahead. Course 060. Four ships, three motor vessels, one escort' the eager listeners heard. Thumbs up! Here was a target worth while – and Wanklyn no doubt felt much as Francis Drake when he spotted a fat-bellied Spanish treasure galleon. He said as calmly as ever:

'Group down. Slow ahead. Stand by one, two and three torpedoes. Up periscope!'

Tension grew as the Commander watched the gratifying spectacle above. If ever there was an answer to fervent prayer, it was here and now. The collection of enemy ships came into the periscope sight. Only the added tensing of Wanklyn's long, lean body told such observers as had eyes for the sight, that this was the moment of decision. The intricate mental calculations that had occupied his mind were incomprehensible to them; but they knew something big was about to happen.

'Fire one. Fire two. Fire three!' Wanklyn said. 'Course 270. Down periscope. Sixty feet!' As quickly as the curt orders were issued they were carried out. *Upholder* turned sharply away from those betraying torpedo-tracks, which would serve as a finger pointing to her position the moment the enemy escort spotted them.

The entire attack had occupied only twelve minutes. Wanklyn claimed no hit, but it is possible the escorts' depth-charges might have drowned the explosion of the impacting missiles. Actually, one hit was scored. With depth-charges bursting around like a firework display, *Upholder* streaked for comparative safety. She was just like a wolf attacking a flock of sheep, snapping at their heels, then bolting away from their protective shepherds. Guerrilla warfare under the sea with a vengeance! Early next morning another ship was sighted to the south. Wanklyn closed in promptly, and through the periscope saw the large red crosses on her side-hospital ship markings of the Sicilian type. Probably he was assured in his own mind that she was packed with munitions and men for Rommel's army; but unlike the enemy, he observed the normal laws of humanity; he gave her the benefit of the doubt, and saw her steam away on her alleged errand of mercy. Thus far the patrol was not proving very profitable, but his patience was endless; he still had a reserve of ammunition, and the gods of the deeper seas would remember him when the hour came around.

They did. Five minutes to noon on 23 May, Wanklyn, his 6 foot 2 inch length cramped in a bunk far too small for him, was called to the periscope. 'Smoke on the horizon,' reported the Officer of the Watch.

'Up periscope,' said Wanklyn in echo. Up it went and yes, sure enough, without shadow of doubt, two motor vessels and one escort were plainly visible.

'Down periscope. Course 300!' he whispered; a course that would bring the killer directly towards the potential victims.

'Diving stations!' rang through the steel hull. 'Stand by one and two tubes!' followed instantly. The control-room, the brain-centre of that small undersea world, sent out its directions to the different compartments. Indicator switches in the control duplicated the orders. The forward ballast pump took a little water from A tank in the bows. The A inboard vent was opened and closed. Perfect equilibrium was established. It was like balancing a rifle to ensure perfect accuracy of aim. And *Upholder* went on closing in on her prey.

'Up periscope!' There was the same baboon-like rising from the crouch on the part of the C.O. There was the zizz as the instrument slid from its housing – an old story, but ever-new, as no one could quite forecast what the ending of the narrative would be. The alert gaze of thirty-four men was concentrated in David Wanklyn's one pair of eyes. All hands were as intent on the outcome as himself. There were beads of sweat on many brows, even a nervous clenching and unclenching of hairy, grimy hands. The control room clock said 1215. The controller of destinies ordered: 'Alter course to 255. Group up. Full ahead.' Then: 'Down periscope.'

This was the critical moment, long hoped-for, the instant when the stealthy stalk ended and the kill began. *Upholder* forged through the water at 9 knots. In her forward compartment the T.G.M. knew nothing of the movements in the control-room, but kept his eyes on the torpedo-firing indicators. Back aft a stoker alertly watched the hydroplane-gear. He knew even less than the T.G.M. about the attack; he was a robot functioning automatically to the bidding of the controlling will. The only thing of which he was conscious was the increased thresh of the submarine's propellers as her speed increased. 'Those also serve who only stand and wait!

'Group down. Slow ahead. Up periscope!' The T.G.M. one hand on the firing lever, saw the word 'Fire' flash on the indicator. His reaction was instantaneous: his hand moved a little, and with that movement his immediate job was completed. One and Two torpedoes were moving to the target, leaving the submarine shuddering as proof that they were on their way.

Course was altered to 170 as Wanklyn heard a torpedo strike the steel hull of the 5,000-ton tanker he had attacked. A murmur of naval praise came from forward and aft: 'Good on you, Wanks!'

'Silence!' the C.O. ordered sternly, knowing that every listening device was trained on his hidden submarine. 'One hundred feet!' The escort destroyer was coming in for vengeance. 'Full ahead' snapped out. 'Silent routine.' The hunter almost in a breath had become the hunted. It was the delicately hung balance of war: this minute to me, that minute to thee.

Whumph! Whumph! Whumph! Eardrums felt like bursting, the hunt was up. Those inboard could hear the queer gurgling whimper of the falling depth-charges long before the pressure detonators caused them to explode with their shattering detonations. Whumph! Whumph! Upholder became flurried in the broken water; she plunged bow-down, then again bow-up, as if she were unable to make up her mind. She writhed, her lean sides moved inwards, then outwards. 'Kind of a blooming concertina!' was how more than one crewman described it afterwards. Cork-chippings showered down from the shivering deckhead, as the glue holding them was shaken loose. Again the jarred light-bulbs dropped to fragmentary ruin underfoot. The venomous attack subsided, but *Upholder* continued to tremble in the frantic water. The steadiest thing aboard was the voice of her Commander ordering: 'Take her down to 150 feet. Shut off shallow water diving-gauges.' Talk about the Rock of Gibraltar for steadiness! The deeper the submarine went the better her momentary immunity and chance of salvation. She dipped her bows slightly; there was an almost unnoticeable tilt of her decks, and as gracefully as a seal, she went deep: 120 feet ... 130 feet ... 150 feet registered on the gauges as she levelled off on an even keel.

'Stop both.' The escort above was listening-hard. An eerie silence answered the command: down there in the half-insulated hull it was possible to hear men breathing, though no bronchial cases were reported among that fit-as-fiddles crew. There was a faint whispering from the still fretful water outside, nothing more. To stop motors doesn't necessarily mean to stop way immediately, but quickly even that murmur ceased, as if the grave had finally closed on this band of living men.

'Escort coming in at high speed!' reported the asdic rating. The beat of her screws was quite audible: an ominous sound.

'Half ahead' showed on the motor telegraphs. Obediently the motor switches splashed home. The submarine was moving. Crash! Whoomph! Anything might happen now. The crew hunched their shoulders as men do in expectation of trouble. But their expectations of the devastating inrush of cold, obliterating water through their boat's split sides didn't materialise. The builders' men at Barrow had been craftsmen, perfectionists. Only the cracking of the absurdly thin plating was evident.

Twenty depth-charges later the men of *Upholder* breathed more freely. Wanklyn's quick thinking and unshakeable calm had baffled the pursuing escort. Once again the dice had rolled in their favour. Accordingly the submarine altered course, to give herself a breathing space to lick her wounds. One of these wounds threatened to have serious consequences. Her listening gear had been put out of action by repeated concussions.

From now onwards until she returned to Malta for repairs she owned no ears to safeguard her from surface attack. The asdic set, acutely sensitive, could not only pick up the sound of shipping at a considerable distance, but could reveal at what angle off the bow it was. In the hands of a skilled operator it could identify the type of ship from the hydrophone effect created by the propellers, and could do this with *Upholder* 150 feet beneath the surface. From now onwards she had only her periscope and visual observation to help her.

While overhead the enemy sub.-chaser wove a fantasy of foaming cat's cradles with its criss-cross wakes, *Upholder* snugged down deep and made the best of the situation.

Finally the attacker departed.

In the noisy interval before this Wanklyn had spent some of the time pondering how to make himself a nuisance, without the necessary equipment, without running too great risks.

His chance came on 24 May. He had barely decided on his selected hunting ground and was waiting for darkness before surfacing. He raised periscope for a quick look-see and only the fact that his hands were busy on the grips stopped him from rubbing them together.

Framed in the periscope were three liners with a strong destroyer escort weaving busy patterns around them. Money for old rope: 'God gives nuts to the man without teeth,' runs the old Spanish proverb.

Upholder had only two serviceable torpedoes remaining. In the half-light, rapidly diminishing, *Upholder* would have to rely solely on sight. Three fat prizes filled the periscope. REAL prizes.

Wanklyn decided to risk it.

CHAPTER 7

FIRST SUBMARINE V.C.

WANKLYN had grown up in the tradition: 'When in doubt engage the enemy more closely.'

After a final look around in the gathering darkness, in which he failed to locate all the destroyers, he started his attack.

'Down periscope. Course 300. Stand by one and two torpedoes.'

He might just as well have said: 'Stand by all torpedoes.' Only two remained. With them, without means of determining whether the destroyers had not already picked him up on their listening devices and were already racing in to attack, he closed in on the liners:

In order to thrust home the attack he would have to come up to periscope depth at intervals and at any moment one of those vague, shadowy destroyers might be waiting to slam her bow through *Upholder's* flimsy shell.

The only warning they would get would be through their ears. And by then it would be too late.

Now it was attack by guess and by God.

The guessing Wanklyn could take care of himself. For the rest? He would rely on the Almighty being in a benevolent mood.

'Up periscope.' The risk had to be taken. His one hope was that failing light might conceal it from the enemy; even though their listening gear was probably as perfect as could be desired.

No one spoke in the eerie silent tension of the control-room. The planesmen were occupied intently on the hydroplanes: Lieutenant Crawford stood between them to oversee their meticulous work. The E.R.A. faced the diving panel. The only absentee was the asdic rating from his useless listening set. Only one voice broke the stealthy silence: the skipper's.

'Three big ones, around 20,000 tons apiece,' he quietly exulted, although fully aware of the startling danger he ran of being rammed by any one of the numerous destroyers.

'Stand by one and two,' he ordered again, to make sure of certainty. One of those shadowy giant hulls was coming neatly into his sights. 'Flood Qs! Eighty feet!' he snapped. Out of this dingy gloom overhead a big destroyer was tearing at top speed towards the *Upholder*, her bow-wave towering like an iceberg ahead of her.

The depth-gauge in the control jumped from 28 to 80 feet as the E.R.A. whipped open Q tank's Kingston valve. A deafening thrashing roar approached the submarine which was for all the world like an express train hurrying through a low tunnel. It surged nearer, menacingly so, and then passed fairly overhead, leaving a churning, boiling welter of water slopping against *Upholder's* casing. That was as near as a toucher!

But no depth-charges. She was on a protective sweep. 'Periscope depth,' said the unmoved Wanklyn. 'Up periscope-steer 295!' *Upholder* stole closer – closer, but even Wanklyn's supernormal vision didn't allow him to see the thousands of enemy troops crowding his target's decks. Reinforcements for the Afrika Korps, almost unlimited!

'Fire one. Fire two!' The control-room clock showed eighteen minutes to nine as the Lieutenant-Commander ordered 'Down periscope. Eighty feet. Course 070' and stood back from his vigilant eye. As the periscope zizzed down into its well he sighed a little, for he had been under an incredible nervous strain.

Crump ! Crump ! Those carefully hoarded torpedoes had not been saved up in vain – far from it. Two 'kippers', two hits: good shooting. And the 17,800-ton troopship *Conte Rosso* was sinking about as rapidly as a ship could sink – she'd got it with a vengeance. In a trice those hordes of reinforcements to ensure victory for Rommel were a panic-stricken morass of shaken humanity. Probably 20,000 fighting men were put out of action in those pregnant seconds when the fate of *Upholder* had quivered in the balance.

There was really no need to worry about shortage of ammunition now. As the *Conte Rosso* dived down, the other troopships turned tail in haste and scudded back whence they had come. They didn't know that the *Upholder's* torpedo supplies were exhausted; they thought the fate that had overtaken their consort must certainly strike them down.

The chagrined destroyers came in for the kill, in a swirl of foam.

Eighty feet below that troubled surface Wanklyn knew that, come what may, he had done his duty well. The cards were stacked heavily against him now from every point of view. He couldn't follow the escorts' movements as he had done on previous hunts, but his absorbed study of every concievable angle of submarine warfare had stood him in good stead. He was steeped in his subject, and had acquired an extra sense that could serve in lieu of sight or hearing: an instinct that is beyond analysis. This action was the supreme test of the man himself, and he had passed it with honours.

The occupants of the control-room watched his face for every change of expression. Such few as were privileged to stand with him in that narrow compartment were highly honoured – and appreciated it. They stood in the presence of greatness.

It is on record that they saw canniness gleaming in his eyes. What impressed them strongly was his ineffable calm: his cultured voice gave no hint of his innermost feelings or thoughts. He was cool, calm, deliberate, they say: the perfect Englishman enveloped in an Englishman's unemotional calm.

Whomtah ! Whomtah! Whump-whump ! How can indescribable sounds be communicated? *Upholder* trembled and kicked like a whale with an electric harpoon in its body as the punitive depth-charges crashed about her. Lights smashed down, cups were jolted from their hooks in the mess-shelves. Buckets rattled; the whole fabric clattered and clashed like a delirious boiler-factory. In the semi-darkness, David Wanklyn gave his course alterations, altered his depth to 100 feet. 'Full speed ahead.' He had to guess the escorts' ensuing moves, pit his extra sense against their diabolically accurate equipment. 'Stop port – slow ahead starboard!' he instructed. The escorts would now be listening hard.

The thresh of a destroyer's screws broke the tension. 'Full ahead both' demanded Wanklyn. 'Eighty feet.' The entombed men heard the depth-charges sizzling towards them seconds before the stunning crash ot their explosions. It was uncanny – to hear potential death go streaking by.

Then the whole of that isolated world shimmered with a blur. They heard another destroyer coming in, another nerve-racking undersea explosion erupted around them, almost shaking their teeth loose in their sockets. The next pattern of depth-charges was almost identical in its effect. It left the men with pounding hearts and fast-rising blood-pressures. Wanklyn was dodging death by hairbreadths. He was creeping away. He had the chasers baffled and bewildered. They were losing contact, their charges were audibly increasing their distance. The wrong scent had been picked up as the wily fox ducked and dodged. Finally a new and secure silence reigned as the enemy lost all touch with that small almost ghostly steel shell beneath the waves.

The recorded depth-charges expended by the enemy numbered thirty-seven. There were probably many more that blended with those more audible. And Wanklyn had dodged the lot, without so much as a whisper reaching his ears from the disabled listening devices. One of the greatest of submariners had proved himself well and truly worthy of the highest decoration 'For Valour'.

He had shattered enemy hopes. He had saved his own crew unscathed. He could return to Base with a satisfied heart.

Back there in Malta, after sinking one of the most valuable prizes recorded – for men were shorter than material – and a laden troopship was a feather in any man's cap – one of *Upholder's* ratings was asked what he thought about the sinking of the *Conte Rosso*. His reply was characteristic of the estimation in which Wanklyn was held by his devoted following:

'That's only the first act for the skipper. Wait till the main event is laid on; then you'll see a few more big 'uns go the same way.'

Another rating said fervently: 'Wanklyn's the finest skipper in the world!' This exuberant way of expressing himself was shared by all his shipmates.

A wag was asked: 'What about all the bounty money you *Upholders* will get after the war? What will you do with it all? In the First World War bounty money at the rate of five pounds per head for all of the enemy put out of action was paid; and at the modest estimate that the *Conte Rosso* was carrying 10,000 troops at least, the total assumed considerable proportions.

The reply came aptly: 'If I live to collect I'm going to buy myself a yacht and have it white-enamelled from stem to stern. Then I'm going to sign on a crew of ex-naval officers and sit back all day watching them wash paintwork!' This spirit of humorous vindictiveness was not characteristic of *Upholder's* men, who had nothing but devoted admiration for the sub.'s officers.

At that time it wasn't known that all prize monies were going to be shared out amongst the entire Navy. It was thought such sums would be distributed to the individual ship or ships concerned. Indeed, in the First World War a submarine's crew sank a large troopship and the humblest rating aboard collected a small fortune. Even Francis Drake's adventurers collected prize-money, and Nelson's toughs believed that this money should be served out in proportion to the shot and shell expended in any given engagement.

So *Upholder's* successful veterans were entitled to indulge in rosy hopes – but it is doubtful if any of them thought they'd live long enough to receive even a trifling share!

Many years have passed since the meagre prize-money was shared out but it is still possible to collect a few rabid opinions on the method of allocation.

Men who put in months, even years of arduous sea time on small ships speak with scorn of men who had 'bobbies' jobs' ashore, but who collected the same amount as themselves.

The caustic comment of one beneficiary, who, hearing of the amount he was to collect, plus the ill-timed official announcement that in future there would be no prize-money at all deserves to be recorded.

'I don't think I'll join the Andrew (The Navy) the next time. I'll go into munitions, then I'll have overtime.' But these were not the thoughts of *Upholder's* crew around this time. They were elatedly conscious of but one thing. Their patrol had paid a handsome dividend. Handsome indeed! With the two last 'kippers' they had sunk a troopship and had sent two others scurrying back home. That was a considerable weight to lift from the struggling British Army ashore.

And it had been done with *Upholder* herself labouring under a handicap.

Although submarines were built to withstand punishment – and did and survived – a comparatively trivial defect could impose a greater handicap on them than on a surface vessel.

A little carelessness or slovenly attention to detail could become a serious matter.

The question of trim was one, for instance, which demanded meticulous care. Without it carried to perfection a submarine might go plunging down out of control, or equally as disastrous might not be able to dive at all before a fresh trim was put on her. With angry surface craft around there was no time for catching up on errors.

An instance of how delicate the trim can be is afforded by this anecdote.

Upholder had stored up, fuelled, taken aboard fresh torpedoes, and all that remained was the matter of trim. Lieutenant Crawford and a Stoker Petty Officer checked all auxiliary tanks, pumping water from some and putting water back into others to compensate for the weight of the fresh stores brought aboard.

Lieutenant Crawford and his assistant came up on the casing well satisfied that everything was in first-rate order below. To their dismay and surprise they found *Upholder* sitting much deeper in the water than was customary.

They exchanged glances, there was the mutual thought. What have we left undone?

Two very worried men went below and religiously re-checked every detail. Everything was as it should be, yet she was sitting too low.

This was serious. She was obviously too heavy somewhere from some undefined cause. A trim dive outside might become anything up to and including a steep-angled dive with little or no control over it.

Crawford reported it to Wanklyn who, in matter-of-fact tones said: 'Don't worry. We'll see how she dives once we're out of the harbour.'

Later, clear of the harbour, Wanklyn ordered: 'Open main vents.' A slow dive was about to take place to check her diving efficiency.

Lieutenant Crawford and the Stoker P.O. were the two most worried men on board. They watched the depth-gauges with considerable apprehension as the vents opened with a dull thud.

And *Upholder* slid under water with the sleek grace of a seal. She was diving and fighting fit for patrol.

The answer, as Lieutenant Crawford found out later, was simple. There had been heavy rain and this in the enclosed creek had altered the density of the water causing her to sit lower than she would have in salt water.

Simple.

Lieutenant Crawford, by the way, left *Upholder* in December 1941 and returned to England to do a Commanding Officer's course. He had a brief spell in H.50, a training boat, then took over P.51, later christened *Unseen*. He returned to the Mediterranean at the end of 1942 and helped to cover the Sicilian landings. He lived up to the Wanklyn spirit by sinking or damaging eleven enemy ships in her.

CHAPTER 8

TARGET: ENEMY CRUISERS

UPHOLDER'S tenth patrol started with disappointments. Three torpedoes were fired vainly at a promising target; no results were obtained, and that piratical beard was stroked more thoughtfully than ever, as its owner pondered over the possible errors he had made. There had been a mistake somewhere, and he puzzled over it with a determination to learn wherein he had failed.

In pursuit of further knowledge, *Upholder* dived at 0415 on 2 July; and as the Commander called: 'Fall out, diving stations' his thoughts were certainly: 'What will today bring in the way of luck?' For success is a heady beverage, breeding a desire for further indulgence.

Just over an hour later the day brought two destroyers, their asdics ping-pinging in acoustic search for under-water craft. But these impulses brought the enemy no intelligence of the British submarine, as Wanklyn and his crew were by now past-masters in the game of hide-and-seek as performed under the Mediterranean's surface.

That day no sleep was lost by the crew, which speaks well for their self-control. Well aware that two viperish destroyers were questing widely in search, eager to kill, the stolid submariners got their heads down to it and their snores outvied the purr of the motors.

This ability to sleep while two destroyers are seeking and listening, eager to come tearing in to blast all hell out of the underseas, is one of the Navy's strong points, inherited, doubtless, from those stalwarts who snatched forty winks between their guns whilst Nelson's ships were bearing down on the French line at Trafalgar.

Wanklyn was reserving his remaining five torpedoes for bigger game than destroyers, and it was obvious to him that such game was practically certain to happen along his line of sight if he but practised patience – a game at which he excelled. Those fretting destroyers were not tearing the seas into froth for fun; they were hoping to clear a safe path for an oncoming convoy; and that expected armada was sure to be ferrying almost unlimited troops or supplies to Africa's burning sands.

Upholder's crew, questioned as to the events of this day, 2 July, indifferently said that it passed uneventfully. At five minutes past four on the morning of 3 July, after a brief spell on the surface, *Upholder* slid smoothly below the sea, her batteries well charged and her interior nicely ventilated. Wanklyn was certain this would prove an eventful day: the restlessness of those destroyers was sufficient proof that big events were pending. His prognostication was, as usual, pretty accurate.

'One supply ship up top!' It was 0640 with a reluctant dawn barely breaking, but sleep was washed from the eyelids as the order: 'Full ahead both' appraised the crew that an attack was in the offing. *Upholder* shook savagely as she did her utmost to get within range, but the supply ship outfoxed her people by the pace she set. A disappointed crew cursed their lack of speed when their Commander broke off what seemed a promising attack. But the enemy undoubtedly felt quite confident, for 1100 brought five ships into the submarine's periscope view, three medium-sized motor vessels, one armed merchant cruiser and one destroyer.

Wanklyn's reaction was: 'Diving stations. Stand by one, two and three torpedoes. Down periscope. Group up! Full ahead, both!' And added almost immediately 'Switch off all unnecessary lights.'

Attack plays havoc with any submarine's batteries, so every ounce of juice must be saved for this most serious work. Click-click went light switches throughout the boat, leaving only the minimum of illumination. The propeller shafts whirled, the eerie half-light seemed to add tension to that already existent.

'Group down. Slow ahead. Up periscope.' Wanklyn's eyes pressed hard to the rubber eyepieces. 'Down periscope!' Only time for a brief, searching glance! 'Steer 120 degrees.' The control-room clock was showing 1115 when he gave that order. Still the tiny vessel shuddered as she closed in, nearer ... nearer. It was 1140 before the Commander was satisfied that he was in perfect range. Tension grew to an almost unbearable extent in that hushed control-room. Then the firm, decisive command sounded: 'Up periscope! Stand by one, two and three.'

'Stand by. Fire one!' Just the lapse of a few seconds, the jarring shiver of the missile leaving the tube, then: 'Fire two. Fire three. Down periscope … Course?' Wanklyn asked casually.

'Course 010,' the helmsman repeated. 'Steer 090. Ninety feet. Half-ahead!' The time was 1142. In all the attack had occupied forty-two minutes. As *Upholder* tilted her bows downwards and gained a depth of 90 feet, at which she levelled off, a torpedo blasted the side of the 6,000-ton *Laura C.* As that revealing waterspout climbed up the doomed ship's side to tower above her funnel, her escorting destroyer swung on her heel, tilting her leeside half-under, and steadying, streaked down the torpedo tracks. Whomph-whamph thundered her depth-charges, but *Upholder's* altered course had done what was necessary. That sharp turn had quite bewildered the pursuer, and the explosions, though shattering a few lights, caused no other damage to the submarine. She appeared to bear a charmed life. In all there had been nineteen of those crashing bursts which gave the impression of tearing the entire sea to whirling froth, but with the diminishing of the din, the hopes of the submariners grew: despite the shaking there was still a fighting chance of a happy ending to yet another patrol. They wiped the cold sweat from their faces and carried on as imperturbably as did the man whose dexterous coolness had saved them to fight another day.

It should be remembered that it was the excellent team-work of all hands that had brought about the serial victories and the almost miraculous escapes; not merely the leadership of one man alone. Wanklyn was the last man alive to claim undue credit for his mastery of the art of destruction; he had trained his men to share his anxieties and his moments of triumph. *Upholder* and crew was a highly tuned instrument on which a master-musician played the dirge of an enemy's approaching humiliation.

Ten hours later the periscope sights spotted a second destroyer searching the area: the enemy had taken the loss of *Laura C* – which had dived down for good – very hard, and the vindictiveness with which the chase continued was proof of the harm that had been done. *Upholder's* men laughed quietly in their sleeves: hate alone wouldn't counteract skill and courage when blended to a perfect pattern.

After five days' further hunting activity, the gallant little boat returned to her Base.

Between 8 and 19 July, her log reads: 'Harbour routine' but even during that period of inactivity, she put out to sea regularly for exercises that would put an even higher polish on her efficiency. Wanklyn was no idle *dilettante*, disposed to rest on his already accumulating laurels, but a perfectionist, always striving after a standard that might well stand as a pattern to the Service he respected so much.

On 17 July, for instance, *Upholder* carried out a dummy attack on her fellow-submarine *Utmost*, also on the anti-submarine trawler *Beryl*: then, tireless in well-doing, on another submarine of her own class, the *Urge*. David Wanklyn's mind conceived every possible circumstance likely to be encountered. He was growing more and more like a master chess-player, who was able to read an enemy's mind like an open book. The essence of his strategy was careful, co-ordinated forethought, by which chance became near-certainty if opportunity arose for the surprise which is the very essence of tactical success.

Not that Wanklyn was selfish in endeavouring to make his command outstanding: he clearly recognised that the game was bigger than the game's player, and he afforded many opportunities to other submarines for similar exercises with the *Upholder* as their target.

All these strenuous and often risky exercises seldom if ever gained publicity; but they were all part of that smooth, silent search for perfection that has for so long characterised the work of the Senior Service, whether surfaced or submerged. Had a working motto been needed to stimulate effort it could have been put tersely: '100 per cent efficiency is only just enough!'

Upholder's eleventh patrol commenced on Saturday, 19 July. At 2200 she sailed, this night-time departure being even a more lonely proceeding than anything that had gone before. She slunk out of harbour as if she were a despicable pariah; no well-wishes sped her going at that hour of creepy gloom, and very tiny and insignificant she appeared to the few silent naval staff who observed her leaving her small world of companionship for the wide open spaces of tensely strung isolation. She was just a dark shadow in a world of blacked-out silence. A humorist aboard the disappearing submarine remarked: 'Saturday night in the Royal Navy!' That said everything. No end-of-week let-up for men who had a duty to perform.

Upholder slipped through the boom into an even darker, more hostile world, an Ishmael of blue-black water, with practically every man's hand against her; her hand against most men – especially such as sailed beneath the arrogant swastika.

Saturday night at sea – 'sweethearts and wives' – was the accepted toast, with the boat's wag bleating out the accustomed corollary: 'May they never meet!' and David Wanklyn, with officers and men alike, re-dedicating themselves to their service – 630 tons of flimsy steel against the colossal might of Germany and Italy combined.

Upholder's complement confidently agreed that whatever happened their way on this eleventh patrol, the enemy would assuredly know that they were abroad again bent on destruction.

The enemy certainly did know it on 24 July, five days after *Upholder* sailed. At 1555 the Officer of the Watch, on raising his periscope for the customary investigation, spotted one motor vessel of 6,000 tons with one lean, rakish destroyer as escort. On the instant Wanklyn took over the periscope, and almost as he sighted the enemy, gave the orders: 'Diving stations. Stand by one, two, and three. Start the attack! Half ahead both. Down periscope!' As the instrument slid down, Wanklyn's eyes flicked down to his watch; the planesman concentrated on the elusive bubble which tells the angle of the submarine as it dives. The attendant stoker's hand was firm on the periscope lever, the mind behind that hand alert for the slightest signal from the specialist in charge of the promised operation. Split-second timing was essential to every soul aboard if the wished – for success was to be theirs again.

Beyond a near-whispered report from the asdic rating, the submarine's interior was now as silent as a long-forgotten grave.

'Up periscope.' It was like a pistol-shot: crisp and decisive.

The stoker pressed his lever; hydraulic pressure shot the periscope upwards with a zizz-z-z. Wanklyn was at the eyepiece long before the upper end emerged from its watery blanket. What he saw was reassuring. What he said was: 'Stand by. Fire one!' Followed the customary shudder. Again: 'Fire two P A bounce. 'Fire three P Bump. Just like that the torpedoes went whining their way towards the condemned motor vessel. There was the inevitable suspenseful wait-seconds seemed to drag by. Waiting was relieved by action. 'Down periscope! Silent routine.'

'Crump !' Ah, there it was: a sound as heartening to the submariner as the clamour of public acclamation. Oh, yes, a definite hit on that desirable target, and a hit pretty certainly meant a sinking. The released suspense was expressed in a general sigh. 'Eighty feet!' decreed Wanklyn, his voice never raised above conversational pitch.

'Destroyer coming in!' said the asdic rating, in a tone as unconcerned and as final as Wanklyn's.

'One-fifty feet!' responded Wanklyn. 'Shut off shallow water gauges.' Upholder seemed to share that stolid calm; she angled down with sweet precision in perfect control. Steady nerves dictated her every movement; there was no disconcerting plunge to indicate panic, simply a smooth downward motion. Even the immediately ensuing Whompta-wompta-wompta-womph didn't cause the crew to bat an eyelid. Not even though Upholder dropped several feet in the partial vacuum caused by the charge-bursts, and then shot up again like an aircraft caught in an air-pocket. All that happened was a change in the direction of the onlookers' gaze: from the composed features of the controller to the sweating deckhead. A water-pressure of 68 pounds to the square inch was bearing on that flimsy upper structure. The almost uncountable depth-charges had exploded immediately overhead, but near though the crashes were, the water did not come cascading in, not even a rivet was chiselled enough to spring a leak. The water-cushion, shallow as it might be, had saved them – for the time being.

The hunted submarine altered course, quickening her speed as the escort vessel came streaking in to attack once more. The ensuing pattern of destruction burst over the conning tower and appeared to be very close. 'By hell, those were near!' commented an unknown voice. Nineteen close bursts in all shook Upholder savagely: her writhings were grotesque. Times were when she appeared to perform a series of somersaults as she bucked and twisted, yet no real harm was done beyond the loss of a few light bulbs and fewer numbers of cups and saucers which had been left off the mess shelf hooks.

The 6,000-ton supply ship sank soon after the torpedo registered in her vitals. This undoubtedly saved Upholder from another handful or so of depth-charges, since the escort had to break off the attack in order to render aid to the crew of this latest victim.

0905 on Sunday 27 July did not find that handful of under-water men at Divisions in No. 1 suits, all spruced up for inspection. Instead it found them going about accustomed duties. In the torpedo-room a working gang of unshaven, unwashed men sweated as they hauled on blocks and tackles to extract a faulty torpedo from No. 4 tube. The stern door of the tube was open, and as they hauled, the missile's propellers came sliding through, then more of the long, blue-tinted cylinder came into view. Down in the forward pump-space, the pump rating saw the indicator light flash its order 'Pump from for'ard'. He started his pump, flashed his signal to control-room: 'Pump started', and, as he saw the vacuum on his gauge, made the signal: 'Pump sucking.' He watched the pump shake on its rubber seating – a precaution against any pump noises being audible outside a submerged hull, which would disclose the presence of a submarine to the delicately balanced listening devices carried by enemy searchers.

He saw the order flash: 'Stop pumping!' That pumping had been necessary on account of extra weight for'ard. In the control-room Wanklyn watched the trim with his usual alertness. He saw the gauge showing 60 feet. The boat was steady and balanced.

For'ard in the torpedo compartment the whole of the sinister-looking 'tinfish' was in full view, warhead and all complete. It looked what it was designed to be: a fearsome tool of destruction, capable of wreaking havoc amongst an enemy's tonnage. From end to end its blue and silver shone almost gaily. The handling crew treated it with reverence, knowing what capacity for the unexpected such weapons are apt to reveal. Out of one unshaven face came: 'Sunday morning in the Andrew!' Another rating cursed the job in hand; there was nothing here at which to cavil: grousing ratings are happy ratings, exercising the Briton's privilege of grumbling even when they have no complaints. 'Grouse you may, go you must' is the password of the lower deck.

The spare torpedo came down from its rack; the condensation drips from the deckhead splashed down on the re-load, as if anxious to mar its deadliness. With encouraging pats from the handlers, wishing it well on its future brief career, the warhead's nose went through the tube door. A haul on the blocks and the 'kipper' (submariner's term for one of the most destructive agents known to man at that period of history), slid gently into place.

The stern-tube door was slammed, clipped shut, and the job was completed to the satisfaction of all concerned, amid a profusion of sighs and gasps from the fore-end men, for hauling back a torpedo of modern size and weight in a confined space, fouled with bad air in a tiny submarine is far from being an easy task. It is a job for experts only, so delicate is the necessary handling. If the torpedo ratings cursed the makers of that faulty kipper, who can blame them?

All this time, 60 feet above their heads, the brilliant sun blazed down on a shining sea: falsely secure.

The Torpedo Officer reported to the Captain: 'Job completed, Sir.' Just another of the day-to-day trials of submarine warfare; in actuality a blessed relief from the corroding monotony. The *Upholder's* log mentions the task casually, a mere routine job, but all the same, muscle, brains and an acid sense of humour were involved.

Wanklyn's extra sense must have been working double-time when he ordered that faulty torpedo-change. At 1940 next day he sighted two cruisers and two destroyers heading towards his periscope. 'Lovely' was his only comment, apart from the order: 'Down periscope.' The big hands were stroked together with a near-loving touch: once again the artist had received inspiration. Not for an instant, however limited his means, did he contemplate avoiding action. To a simple man the course of duty is a straight line – hit as hard as you can, and damn the consequences!

'Diving stations' Wanklyn called. On its heels: 'Stand by all tubes.' He waited until all were at stations before mentioning: 'Two cruisers, two destroyers up top!' and the waiting ratings reacted accordingly. One such matlow, looking like a kerbside wastrel, murmured: 'Lovely grub!'

Wanklyn took a snap-look through the periscope, wasting no time. As the column slid down to its seating, he rubbed his big hands slowly together. This time he was pitted against the keen wits of specialist-trained fighting men: it was a game of chess on a board as wide as history.

Maybe he thought of the cruisers' commanders. Were they like so many of their type who said, after the hectic days of 1914-18 had ended: 'Undersea boats have had their day. They are as obsolete as muzzle-loading 64-pounders.' The kind of arrogant boasters who said: 'Take that dirty stinking submarine away from my ship's side.' If Wanklyn thought along such lines it might account for the slightly sardonic expression on his bearded, mobile features. He waited to open his attack.

'Up periscope!' A swift glance brought them into view like the objects on a camera view-finder: diminished but clearly defined. The destroyers were zigzagging at high speed on either bow of the big ships, weaving a foamy defence around their more vulnerable charges. The cruisers were pushing high waves before their sharp bows as they forged purposefully ahead. In that brief glance Wanklyn selected his target: the Italian cruiser *Garibaldi*. Mussolini's navy stood to lose one of the jewels of its crown. Wanklyn wiped the moisture from the eyepiece, steamed up like a motor-cyclist's goggles. Another satisfying glance and then: 'Down periscope!' Sixty pregnant seconds ticked by on the control-room clock. 'Up periscope.' Deep silence reigned there in the boat's nerve-centre. The mind behind that face was concentrated on the *Garibaldi*, and how best to strike her a mortal blow. A well-built cruiser was something different from a troopship: *Upholder* was going to attempt to engage the unsinkable. Multitudinous compartments assured her buoyancy; her vulnerable parts were armoured with chilled steel. Having settled with himself the best course to adopt, deciding that the *Garibaldi* was now in position for the coup: 'Fire one, two, three and four! Down periscope.'

Four successive, outsize hiccoughs shook *Upholder* as the torpedoes parted company with her, to speed quickly and truly, leaving their pencil-lines as evidence of their presence in the war-zone.

'Eighty feet.' As the order went into effect Wanklyn complemented it by another: 'Course 90 degrees!' *Upholder* swung at right angles to the line-of-run of the torpedoes, and those aboard her waited … one minute, two minutes, three minutes. Any second now might bring the heartening crump of a hit. Hearts were racing, despite iron control. Mouths gave odd little twitches; all, perhaps except the mouth of the man of steel himself. Hit or miss, his expression remained immobile as that of the sphinx.

Four minutes, and … crump, crump! Two hits for certain. The first action against powerful war-vessels had been successful. Wanklyn's eyes twinkled. His lean fingers caressed the famous beard with the gratified gesture of a successful artist.

The *Garibaldi* stopped dead in its tracks as the two torpedoes tore into its bows. One destroyer quickened speed to head down the frothy tracks, the other, smoke belching from its funnels, streaked round the stricken craft, locking the stable door too late; but the heavy smoke screen it laid promised a screen from a further, shattering attack.

Destroyer Number One raced directly and immediately over the *Upholder*, shooting its depth-charges in all directions to encompass as wide a sea-area as might be. The sea shimmered; great mounds of sea-water formed, rose, broke into towering waterspouts. They seemed to reach for the sky. Down below, in 80 feet of cushioning water, the screws of those hurrying avengers caused *Upholder*'s crew to hunch their shoulders more than a little, just as the thud-thud of the depth-charges turned their hearts over with their menace. The thresh of overhead activity stopped. The pursuer was listening, listening hard. *Upholder* stopped. The desperate game of hide-and-seek was well away.

'Destroyer coming in at speed!' called the man at the asdic set.

'Full ahead both,' snapped Wanklyn. Only those who have actually experienced this blind groping and chasing can imagine the atmosphere created within the pursued vessel. It isn't informed with fear because there is no fear that can do full justice to the situation. You cannot be scared enough, so all that emotion is washed up into a semi-nonchalance that numbs the faculties and causes the subconscious to register: 'Who cares? Hell's bells. Press on regardless.' And then, as the numbness eases the following emotion takes charge: 'Isn't the skipper looking confident?' That meant you were escaping – for the time being anyhow, and tomorrow would be another day.

All those thirty chunks of potential destruction had practically scraped *Upholder's* hide, but, behold, they'd got away... and the *Garibaldi* was lying badly damaged off Marritimo.

Wanklyn waited until three minutes past ten that night and then blew *Upholder's* main ballast-tanks, surfacing in the Stygian darkness. Nothing menacing appearing, she zigzagged her way to quieter waters before diving at midnight or just a little while before. Once submerged the torpedo, a Mark VIII, which had been drawn out of No. 4 tube on the Sunday, was re-loaded – it was the only fang remaining of all her teeth.

She surfaced again soon after midnight, and a happy band of men rejoiced openly. All was quiet. The glorious fresh air was roaring bracingly down the conning tower. Exhilaration grew. These long-immured tough men could now celebrate victory by inhaling lungfuls of the cigarette-smoke they had been so long denied. Life was good indeed.

But there was no rest for the crew, not with a dedicated Captain who still had one torpedo remaining, even if it had needed a little patching up. A doubtful weapon, but it might function, and so long as such a hope remained, Wanklyn esteemed it his duty to quest in search of further prey.

At 0320, the night alarm sounded. The ratings bounced to their stations. Wanklyn had sighted a convoy: four motor vessels and three destroyers. Indomitably he closed in to attack with his one shaky torpedo, and damn the consequences!

'Stand by one torpedo!' Almost a pitiful order with such a promising armada in sight.

0335 came, and *Upholder* plunged below the surface: at 0346 she emerged once more and Wanklyn shot to the drenched bridge in an instant to estimate the situation, and instantly, to order 'Fire!'

Wasted effort! No hit was claimed for that questionable missile. More likely than not it failed to run true. It conceivably did hit – there is no proof to the contrary; but the perfectionist never claimed success if even a shadow of doubt remained. This was the luck of the game. Dawn began to streak the sky, and, no longer a unit fit for combat, *Upholder* dived, then set a course for home.

All next day two destroyers searched the area with the purposefulness of a nurse combing her charge's hair. Wanklyn watched them as they searched, his periscope moving up and down as the situation demanded. It was a thoroughly comprehensive sweep the enemy made, but not quite thorough enough to prevent *Upholder* entering Malta Harbour just before dusk on the last day of July.

She received a welcome of rousing cheers as she tied up in No. 3 berth, Lazaretto, her Jolly Roger flying triumphantly high, her success bars mounting high on the flag's black background. *Upholder* was proudly home, and prouder than any man aboard her was Captain 'Shrimp' Simpson, rejoicing in the fact that his ace submarine had returned-intact and once again victorious.

CHAPTER 9

CLOAK AND DAGGER

ON Friday, 15 August, H.M. submarine *Upholder* took in a special parcel of cargo, additional to her normal stores of rations, rum and torpedoes. Some of her crew wondered what in Hades was coming next! This was not a torpedo. It was a long and narrow canoe-shaped gadget made of pliable rubber. But, since it was a war of wonders, the ratings not in the know merely shrugged. Anyway, it would be all right. This strange intruder was a folboat (rubber canoe), devised for special hush-hush operations. Accompanying it were obvious demolition charges. Certainly some new and astonishing escapade was afoot.

Another submarine patrol was about to start: everything was in an advanced state of preparation. Stores were stowed away in their appointed lockers, the fuel tanks brimmed. The torpedo tubes were loaded with a full salvo, and the racks forward housed a sufficiency of re-loads – if ever Wanklyn felt he had a sufficiency. This man was never satisfied with the destructive quality of his command: like Oliver Twist he always pined for more, even though the cramped hull was crowded to capacity.

The crew came through the hatches with the ease of long familiarity, joking as they passed under the casing. But they still wondered what the presence of that rubber oddment might foretell, even as they dumped their steaming-bags in their appointed tiny messes. Any other type of humanity than a submariner would have wondered exceedingly how existence in such cramped space was a possibility.

Almost on the edge of sailing-time the mystery began to solve itself. Two unusual passengers came aboard, one Army Lieutenant, one Army

Corporal. They weren't there as pleasure-passengers, assuredly: their general get-up foretold stern business.

Conjecture went by the board as 'Harbour stations' echoed through that overcrowded hull. 'Uncotter main vents' succeeded. The cotter-pins were withdrawn from the main ballast-tank vents, each compartment sending its orders by word-of-mouth to the control-room. The reports came into that brain-centre like hail: 'Engine-room hatch shut and clipped', 'Fore hatch shut and clipped'. The two passengers listened, half-understanding, to these interludes in a jargon unfamiliar to their ears. Telegraphs jangled, the propeller shafts turned, the steering-gear whined and *Upholder* was under way once more to make a rendezvous with Destiny.

Malta faded away as *Upholder's* propellers pushed her resolutely towards the Sicily area where her orders demanded her presence. Something of the nature of a cloak-and-dagger show seemed to be in the offing.

The weather was hot and calm. The look-outs wore casual dress, open-necked shirts, and were over-warm even so. For once Wanklyn had discarded his uniform jacket.

Inside that narrow hull many were stripped to the waist; beads of sweat clung to hairy chests. By this time the passengers were known by name: the Army Officer was Lieutenant Walker of the Hertfordshire Regiment; the Corporal was named Bird, of the Beds. & Herts. Regiment. Both were 'special operations' experts attached to submarines.

Wanklyn welcomed the officer cordially: he loved a game of bridge, and as normally only four officers were aboard, one of whom was on watch and not available during every patrol, no opportunity arose for indulgence in his pastime. Thus the advent of the extra officer was in its way a godsend.

Wednesday, the 20th, brought minor excitement when at four minutes to nine, one 2,000-ton motor vessel, escorted by one trawler, was spotted heading towards *Upholder*.

That called for action. 'Diving stations. Stand by one and two torpedoes' was instantly ordered. The submarine's raised periscope left a distinct trail on that placid sea-surface, so Wanklyn ordered it to be lowered. Minutes went by. The *Upholder* closed distance and in the immediate keenness the smell of hot, sweating bodies went unnoticed.

The time was 0931. The white feathery periscope wake was again above *Upholder's* decks. The 2,000-tonner was coming neatly into the line of fire.

'Fire one. Fire two!' snapped Wanklyn. Obediently two missiles streaked from the submarine's bows, like pilot fish escorting a man-eating shark. The enemy ship staggered and shook as a high column of foam-topped water lifted skywards, and a terrific explosion seemed likely to destroy the submarine as well as her victim. It was kaput for that target: she sank within a very few minutes and left merely a greasy smear on the water. The escorting trawler hurried down the torpedo-tracks, depth-charges at the ready and already dropping them. *Upholder* went on with the old familiar routine; shivering and shaking hard as the explosions crashed around her. She altered course smartly and bafflingly. She had dodged attack once again, and her crew began to exult – here was the first outright kill of the new patrol. Here was a good omen for the coming days.

On Friday, the 22nd, Wanklyn's eyes took on their customary glint of expectation as from 28 feet below the surface his periscope disclosed the promising prospect of three motor vessels and three destroyers. It was 1545. The day was a Friday and it promised to be unlucky for someone: the crew felt sure it would be the enemy who took the count. One destroyer to one supply ship! That showed how valuable the convoy was.

'Stand by one, two, three, and four torpedoes' was Wanklyn's immediate reaction to this promising sight. The submarine was at once a hive of activity, all of it purposeful. The mere tone of that commanding voice told all within hearing that something big was astir. The telegraphs rang 'Half ahead'. A hush descended on the control-room; only Wanklyn's instructions broke it. The Commander's attack team waited with bated breath: they were tense as a harp-string, awaiting that pregnant word 'Fire!'

Wanklyn was thrusting his head into the lion's mouth with a vengeance.

At 1630 his expression grew even more concentrated and serious. The wan light reflected from the periscope mirrors gave his eyes an uncanny gleam.

Through his periscope he saw one destroyer on the engaging bow. The order to fire was shaping on his lips when he saw this destroyer slip astern of the convoy. He had accurately estimated this move, for the time being he appeared to have projected his mind into the thoughts of the enemy.

The tension snapped like pack-thread when the order: 'Fire one, two, three, and four!' was given. The critical moment had arrived after a seemingly interminable wait by the thirty-four submariners. Six tons of torpedoes were flung out into the seas; as they left the tubes *Upholder's* course was altered violently, away from the tell-tale tracks.

Crump, crump sounded with startling clarity. Two hits! Excellent shooting: two out of four was a good average bag. The 4,500-ton tanker hardly knew what hit her. In double-quick time she dived like a plummet to the Locker and that was her finish.

A very angry destroyer came streaking towards the dived submarine. Her plentiful depth-charges tore the under-water world to fury. *Upholder's* crew had the feeling that they were inside an outsize boiler, with the world's biggest steam-hammer trying to split its seams apart.

Wanklyn again altered course, and, as the attacker steamed in, speeded up his own motors. The charges buzzed down, and, as they burst, the whole immediate area shivered and trembled. Inside Wanklyn's boat the usual phenomena occurred: lights flickered, left their sockets, plopped to splinters underfoot. There was a shower of glass fragments, a cascade of cork chippings, with an ominous swish of water swirling around the sub.'s casing. There followed a silence that was as if specially designed by Nature to add to the drama. Here and there the quick thumping of an overstrained heart was audible – nothing more, until Wanklyn ordered: 'Half ahead both – 150 feet.' The hunted submarine tilted down smoothly, hastened on her descent by the following pattern of charges which forced her down still deeper and more quickly.

It was 1950 before Wanklyn pushed up his periscope to discover a Spica-class destroyer hurrying away from that hellish vicinity like a scalded cat-28 knots he estimated her speed. Probably she had exhausted her depth-charge reserves and feared reprisals!

A brief respite was permitted them. On Sunday morning *Upholder* lolled lazily at periscope depth, for all the world as if observing a carefree Sabbath with never a care in the world. At 1020 Wanklyn shoved up his periscope and swept the whole circle of the horizon, then checked again.

His loyal crew vowed that even when dead asleep his extra sense kept him informed of the imminence of action. For hardly was the periscope up and steady than: 'Diving stations' was commanded. It sounded through the boat with an even greater urgency than usual.

That suggestion of vital urgency caused a dozen voices to question: 'What is it – what?' And the answer was quite simple. In the periscope's range of vision showed one battleship, two cruisers, and six destroyers: an answer sufficient to satisfy the most curious rating who ever scrubbed a deck or washed a soiled vest.

'Darned hard luck for the skipper!' was the general verdict. Here was a miniature armada, waiting for the torpedoes to damage and destroy – and there were only two torpedoes left.

'Down periscope. Stand by torpedoes,' Wanklyn ordered, as cool and deliberate as ever he had been. His boat vibrated tremulously as she closed in to the kill.

1035 – and it was now or never. Very soon the promising targets would be out of range. Even now the distance was considerable, making accurate shooting rather more difficult than usual, for torpedoes are occasionally extremely temperamental. 'Up periscope.' The real battle gleam was in Wanklyn's eyes. He grabbed the handles of the periscope; waited until the wash on top cleared as the eye burst through that dazzling, sun-washed sea. There were nine warships within his range of vision. What a haul – if only – !

'Fire one. Fire two. Down periscope. 150 feet. Silent routine!' Quick orders, quietly and quickly obeyed. Not even this critical moment brought a tremor to that controlled voice – and it promised to be as great a moment as any in Wanklyn's busy life. Every man-Jack below knew that his life would immediately be dependent on that skipper who believed in attempting the impossible whenever a chance occurred. Only silence, immediate obedience to every quick command, with every order executed at the double, could afford them the best immunity from deadly retribution.

The destroyers roared towards *Upholder* like blooded greyhounds, hiding themselves in their own bow-waves and wake-wash. There was a savage threshing of hurrying propellers overhead, a rustling of water, and then – a shattering series of deafening, ear-splitting explosions that seemed like the end of all creation. The submarine bucked and plunged. Her interior became as blurred as a television picture out of focus. Again and again the depth-charges cascaded down, and with the last vicious pattern Upholder's crew fancied the end had already come. The last pattern was so ominous that its racket chilled their blood, bringing out ice-cold drips of uncontrollable sweat on their brows.

Forty-eight close depth-charges later, they began to hope that life might be theirs again, after all. The enemy destroyers had left the scene of action. Maybe they thought they had made a decisive kill. It may have been that they concentrated their efforts to assist a sadly battered cruiser, for *Upholder's* log recorded a possible, even a probable hit on a ship of that type. The flurry of action prevented too accurate an estimate.

The submarine glided up from her 150-feet concealment. The asdic rating listened intently: no suspicious sounds came from up on top. Her periscope broke surface and Wanklyn took a comprehensive look round the horizon. He saw nothing beyond a clear, sunny sea. The control-room clock was still functioning normally, despite the upheavals that had shaken the submarine like a half-set jelly. A good advertisement for its makers. It registered 1220. As Wanklyn ordered: 'Blow main ballast-surface,' the air screamed through the air-lines into the ballast tanks; amid a cascading swirl of bubbles, *Upholder* shook the water from her back. Lookouts leaped smartly to their posts on the bridge; the wireless operator sent his message – one of the greatest importance, for it was a report of the enemy squadron's position and course – a useful guide to our surface Navy and to the R.A.F. based on Malta.

Eighteen minutes later, at 1248, the submarine dived. She had chanced her luck by a surface appearance of more than a quarter of an hour in broad daylight in enemy waters, incurring great risk to all on board.

The following day, *Upholder*, with her torpedo tubes and spare torpedo racks empty as a swept barn, surfaced at 2108 and immediately closed in towards the Sicilian coast; her destination the first bay to the eastward of Cape Palermo. She closed the land very slowly, so as not to leave a distinguishable, betraying wake. Her hull was trimmed well down. Mediterranean phosphorescence can be very vivid and revealing to sharp-eyed observers overhead. Within fifteen minutes of midnight the lookouts could smell the shore – a characteristic odour. A minute or so later they could see the enemy land – it showed clear as a picture on a cinema screen. A critical operation was impending.

Down below in the fore-ends Lieutenant Walker and Corporal Bird were dressed to go ashore. Their faces were grotesquely blackened and they wore thickly rubbered shoes. Tommy-guns and Commando knives formed their offensive armament. Their folboat was in immediate readiness to be lifted to the casing, and plentiful demolition charges were by their sides, carefully nursed.

At five minutes to twelve Wanklyn whispered down the voice-pipe: 'Stop both.' The barely turning propellers came to a dead halt and the submarine carried her way for only a little distance. The fore-hatch was opened and the folboat passed through to the casing. Every operation was performed in a profound hush.

At one minute to midnight the fore-hatch was closed, leaving the folboat and demolition charges on the casing. But it was 0010 on Tuesday, 26 August, that Walker and Bird floated away from the submarine, their paddles clipping in hushed silence into the flat, calm water. The darkness enveloped them as if they had never been. On *Upholder's* bridge Wanklyn watched and listened with all alertness. He whispered: 'They'll be ashore now', and as if his words were being echoed, a crackle of revolver shots from the shore appeared to give definite answer. All on the submarine's bridge heard loud, alarmed shouting from the land, and the yelping and barking of mongrel dogs suddenly aroused them. Bullets from a couple of rifles hit the water close alongside the intruding submarine. Something was obviously wrong ashore. It looked as if the game was up before being properly started.

Wanklyn didn't know what was happening, naturally enough, but what actually occurred was that the two cloak-and-dagger enthusiasts had managed to hide their boat, prior to striking inland, carrying their demolition charges very tenderly. They hoped they might be able to lay them on the tracks of the South Sicilian Railway.

After an hour of taut suspense, *Upholder* was still close inshore. Wanklyn, judging by the audible evidence, was practically certain the party had met with total disaster, but he still went on hoping and waited patiently for events. He had to be sure – he was always that way. He left nothing to chance if it were possible.

Meanwhile, ashore, Walker and Bird had climbed for an arduous hour. It was a very stiff climb they had to effect, and the toughness with which they tackled it showed great devotion to duty on their part, carrying on, laden with high explosives. Meantime a strong search party was combing the landscape in hope of discovering them. It was after an hour's toil that the pair noticed a train which was still a mile away. The charts they had studied so meticulously were completely wrong. Lieutenant Walker, knowing that *Upholder* was only three miles away from the fishing town of Sciacca, which was more than possibly a base for E-boats, decided to return to the submarine, whereupon the two men buried their charges carefully, and started on the road back to the beach base.

Wanklyn went on waiting. One-thirty came – slow minutes of waiting, as torturing as the swiftest action. Still the dogs yapped and howled in the near-distance. Shouts were clearly audible: what all this clamour portended could only be estimated. Apprehension naturally bred odd fancies: at any moment a high-speed E-boat might come hurtling through the surrounding gloom; or a bracket of shells from a shore-battery make the night hideous. Anything could happen – anything.

Another endless quarter of an hour dragged by, and still no boat appeared or gave evidence of its nearness. One hour and a half had elapsed since this stage of the operation had commenced. Fears grew and enlarged amongst those who waited; a sureness that the whole enterprise was a hopeless flop. The best to be expected was that Walker and Bird were prisoners-of-war; the worst, that they had met with a quick and merciful death.

Ten minutes more – would this tension never slacken? Silent and immobile as a ghost-ship *Upholder* waited ... With time passing so slowly even the normally patient Commander was moved to whisper frequently down the voice-pipe for a record of the passing minutes. And the two adventurers had meanwhile reached the beach, found their hidden boat and were cautiously paddling back.

'What's that?' It was more a thought than a question? The cause of it was a feeble blue flickering torch-signal: the folboat's recognition flash. The exhaled breath of those who saw it was almost loud enough to startle the sleeping Sicilians, if any were still asleep. Within five more minutes the flimsy landing-craft was snugly stowed on the submarine's casing.

By 0214 the folboat and all the rest of the soldiers' impedimenta was in place below decks, and within another five minutes the fore-hatch was shut and clipped. *Upholder* then proceeded to open water-always moving with silent caution.

According to his usual custom, David Wanklyn had performed a perfect job for those relying on his services. For a period of over two hours he had held his submarine in instant readiness, so close to a hostile shore that it was possible to hear the splashes from rifle shots, fired at random, and which had washed down his exposed bridge casing. Sure proof how close he had been to the land.

On Wednesday, 27 August, *Upholder* entered harbour once again, carrying a happy crew in a riotously exultant mood. No wonder they rejoiced: two certain kills to their credit and an almost certain hit on a fast and powerful cruiser.

CHAPTER 10

THIRTEENTH PATROL

THE question troubling the minds of *Upholder's* crew was: would a thirteenth patrol prove unlucky? Even in a press-button, near-atomic age, old-time superstitions still prevail in the Royal Navy, and this number had always been chosen by seamen as the unluckiest of all. To submarines, all days and dates could be overwhelmingly unlucky, of course, but as Wanklyn's command readied herself for sea, the figure 13 seemed to stand out on every bulkhead.

Hard work, however, kept the men from dwelling too morbidly on the possibilities, even though they had so often seen fellow-submariners depart from moorings in the Creek, fade away into the darkening horizon, and vanish, never to be seen or heard of again.

Fresh torpedoes were taken aboard to replace those so usefully expended, and handling these missiles allowed little time for reflecting on past glories or future horrors. It was a repetitive case of nose to the grindstone. The submarine base at Malta possessed few luxuries. There were no foam-baths, sun-ray lamps and such like devices for toning up the human system. No idle loafing for the *Upholders*, with glamorous Wrens to minister to their every need. Neither officers nor men were indulged with fancy diets to titillate war-jaded appetites; they got just what the rest of the island got, being rationed rigorously even to the amount of ordinary bread they ate – one slice per meal, and if that didn't suffice, well – they went hungry!

The ratings bathed in a bucketful of the hardest water imaginable: little enough of an improvement on sea-water; a whole packet of soap powder was needed to brew up even the semblance of a lather, and even then, an irritating stickiness of the skin remained to destroy any feeling of real cleanliness.

The Submarine Service fought on, and the human element continued to grin and bear it. There were no brass bands and waving banners to herald their arrivals; no garlands were draped about their necks. Their average life was unnoticed and unrecorded, but the frantic heads of Italian and German Services knew to their cost just what their value was.

Upholder's crew refused to worry even if this thirteenth patrol was coming up. No time for worry, come to think of it. Two days after entering port on 27 August, the submarine under Wanklyn's command was once again ready to resume the offensive and about to proceed to sea.

1855 saw her springs being cast off. It saw David Wanklyn, recuperated and vigorous as ever, back on his bridge. It saw the now famous submarine's bows pointed seawards without even a hint of fuss or flurry: just a few friendly voices calling 'Good luck, David!' and 'Good hunting!' And such hails were answered merely by a brief wave of one big, skilful hand. A rating at the Base shouted to his buddy on Upholder's casing 'All the best!' Scant as these farewell calls might be there was nothing half-hearted about them; they were as sincere as the hopes of further victory that animated all hearts aboard *Upholder*. She was lost to view before Captain 'Shrimp' Simpson turned slowly away.

Saturday passed uneventfully enough. On Sunday morning at five o'clock *Upholder* dived under, dipping down gracefully like a seal, in perfect trim. The sea was as bare as the palm of Wanklyn's hand.

At 0637 her inquisitive periscope broke surface, and expectant eyes spotted nine ships: three motor vessels and six destroyers, to prove exactly how jittery the Italians were growing: a six-ship escort for three supply ships.

One glimpse of the target was enough to cause Wanklyn, closing in already, to order 'Full ahead', and to set those hands rubbing together in smooth satisfaction. The distance separating prey from hunter was great. *Upholder's* control-room was hot and sticky, this being the height of the Mediterranean summer. Men dripped sweat as if emerging from a bath. Breathing was none too easy.

'Stand by all tubes. Slow ahead.' Then came 'Fire all tubes!' At 0710 the torpedoes left their housing. Perhaps because it was the thirteenth patrol, of all that flock of missiles not one registered a claimable hit. The nine ships continued their urgent voyage without apparently suffering casualties. The hoodoo thirteenth patrol ended with the submarine arriving back at Base the following day, 1 September. It had been what the submariners termed a 'blitz patrol' – a quick, unblooded excursion.

Upholder's fourteenth patrol commenced on Tuesday, 16 September, and within twenty-four hours she was in contact with her three companion submarines: *Upright, Ursula,* and *Unbeaten.* All were under orders to intercept a large enemy troop convoy, consisting of three of the enemy's largest and finest liners: *Neptunia, Oceania,* and *Vulcania* (each around 20,000 tons). They carried vital reinforcements for Rommel's army. With these additional troops Rommel would, in all probability, overwhelm his opponents and assure a triumphant victory in North Africa. But on this September day they still had to get by David Wanklyn and his crew, and the crews of *Ursula, Unbeaten,* and *Upright.*

On this occasion *Upholder* was labouring under a severe handicap; her gyro-compass had failed and she was dependent on her magnetic compass which did not guarantee the same certainty of manoeuvre the disabled instrument would have done.

At 0300 on the 18th *Upholder* was trimmed down to 'casing-awash' – with just her conning tower visible above the sea's surface. The First Lieutenant, Lieutenant M. L. C. Crawford, was Officer of the Watch. Two for'ard look-outs scanned the sea closely for any sign of the expected convoy or the sharp bows of an escorting destroyer which might upset all Wanklyn's carefully laid plans.

The asdic rating received a signal from *Unbeaten,* lying to the eastward, reporting the convoy approaching towards *Upholder's* 'billet', as the area of a submarine's patrol is named. Wanklyn received this message from the control-room messenger, and he immediately joined Crawford on the bridge.

'Call diving stations, Number One.'

'Diving stations … diving stations … diving stations!' Crawford shouted down the voice-pipe. As his voice reached the control-room it re-echoed throughout the entire structure of the boat: 'Diving stations … diving stations … diving stations': all hands closed up to their allotted stations. All men were now on watch: torpedo crew in the torpedo compartment, coxswain and second coxswain in the control-room, extra hands in the motor-room and engine-room: every man-Jack on the alert, with hearts thumping with excitement, and blood pressure rising like a thermometer in a heat wave.

Upholder closed in towards the nine ghostly shadows – that is all they were – the coxswain finding great difficulty in maintaining a steady course because of the damaged gyro-compass – nine dim shapes moving through the darkness and the choppy seas, with never a glimmer of phosphorescence to betray them in certain detail. Wanklyn and Crawford strained their eyes through the night-glasses, intent on estimating the speed of the nearing transports.

Wanklyn still closed in, tension increasing inside the dank interior of his command. The Engine Room Artificer on the diving panel was ready to send *Upholder* plunging into the depths on receipt of the three vital words: `Dive .., dive ... dive!' In the fore-ends the Torpedo Gunner's Mate stood ready to pull the levers that would start his torpedoes on their deadly run.

Upholder closed in at 12 knots-full speed – but too far away to fire with the absolute certainty Wanklyn demanded.

The sub. was drawing very close to the destroyer escort: six vicious killer-ships, weaving in and out like figures in a ghostly dance, their look-outs as vigilant as any on the *Upholder's* bridge; their asdic listeners equally intent. Still *Upholder* closed in, nearer ... nearer. It was now or never; the target ships would be drawing away out of effective range in a trice. The speed of the big fellows approximated 27 knots; the escorts were making a full 35 knots.

'Stand by Nos. one, two, and three torpedoes!' came the curt order from the bridge. All indicator lights showed the green stand-by light. And then, from the bridge: 'Fire one!' The flick of the switch in the control-room flashed the command. The green light for'ard changed to red – with the word 'Fire' black against its glow. This was the most exciting moment of all – the strain of keyed-up waiting was broken.

The T.G.M. pulled the firing lever. Number one torpedo shuddered from its tube. *Upholder* seemed to pause for a fraction of a second; number one was speeding fast and true towards the troopships. A few seconds later: 'Fire two!' – the same flick of green to red, the same shudder ... and number two was on its deadly mission. 'Fire three!' came a few seconds later. Three torpedoes were running beneath the choppy surface, each carrying a warhead of some thousand pounds of T.N.T. A 5,000-yard run and four minutes waiting, breathless waiting for Wanklyn and his crew.

'All below!' rasped Wanklyn. The look-outs scrambled down the conning-tower trunk. Lieutenant Crawford followed them in orderly haste.

'Dive. Dive. Dive!'

The E.R.A. ripped open the main vents, and *Upholder* was dipping downwards. Wanklyn stayed on the bridge, hoping to see with his own eyes the torpedoes strike home.

'Come on down, Sir ... come on down, Sir' shouted Crawford. Wanklyn almost reluctantly left the bridge, pulling the hatch shut overhead, and clipping it fast precisely as he heard the rush of water covering the conning tower.

'Blow Q-tanks,' ordered Crawford, to arrest too quick a descent. There was a hiss of air, and the indicator showed 'Q tanks empty'.

'Stop blowing,' commanded Number One. They planed down still deeper. Silence hung like a pall inside the *Upholder*. Seconds seemed like hours, minutes like days to Wanklyn, who had pitted all his careful knowledge, daring and skill against a by-no-means-to-be-despised enemy, it felt that years were slowly passing by.

On the success or failure of those three missiles depended the lives of thousands of British fighting men ashore.

Two minutes! A slight fidgeting took place throughout the boat. All eyes watched the clocks. Three minutes! Any second now, with luck, would come the dull knocking note of the first hit. It didn't come. Sweat-beads formed on their foreheads, a choking sensation in parched throats as each man began to swallow convulsively.

Almost four minutes – those clock-hands seemed paralysed by the suspense. And then – 'Crump!' Number one torpedo had found its target. 'Crump!' and then by all the powers above, 'Crump' again. Three hits out of three-a trio: was ever such shooting experienced before? The impossible had happened.

And from stem to stern: 'Good old Wanks!' came the heartfelt praise from men who had every reason to be proud of such first-rate leadership. For this was the moment that made all the hardships, discomforts and dangers more than worth while.

Not that *Upholder* knew at that moment how vital her success had been. Those inboard were mainly aware of the thresh of the hunters' propellers, as chagrined destroyers whirled and spun to and fro overhead, questing their invisible enemy that had struck such a disastrous blow.

Waiting for what seemed to be the inevitable depth-charge attack bred that cold stark anticipatory fear that numbs human thought. It says much for human fortitude and the quality of submarine personnel that such emotions are never allowed to take charge.

At this time the *Upholder's* crew did not know what had happened around them: that the 20,000-tonner *Neptunia* had already found final anchorage in Davy Jones' Locker. When the expected depth-charge attack failed to eventuate, the idea grew in the crew's mind that some definite result had been achieved, that depth-charges dared not be dropped for fear of destroying enemy human life.

'Blow main ballast! Surface!' Wanklyn ordered. His subordinates considered him ready for the madhouse; but Wanklyn had to see for himself what the result of his calculated attack had been. Merely listening to the crumps of the exploding torpedoes wasn't sufficiently satisfying to his intense curiosity.

He opened the conning-tower hatch and scrambled up to the bridge. Through the night-glasses, in the still prevailing gloom, he saw one troopship stopped dead, one streaking away, flat out on power, and the signs of one sunk. One enemy on the bottom, one seriously damaged.

'Dive ... dive ... dive!' he commanded. *Upholder* slid below the surface, without even the questing destroyers spotting her. Wanklyn had that feeling of victorious achievement, plus the tinge of regret that touches all men who win victory at the cost of human life. He was no cold-blooded assassin delighting in killing for killing's sake; but he knew that *Upholder* had saved and was still saving the lives of uncounted fellow-countrymen ashore on Africa's scorching sands, and he was elated.

He took his submarine down 60 feet or thereabouts, and headed south. *Upholder* was not running away from combat, but was heading for quieter waters in order to re-load her torpedo tubes. A torpedo, weighing in the average 30 cwt. or so, is no small weight to handle from the racks in confined space, but at 60 feet in quiet water *Upholder* was steady enough to permit a safe and fairly sheedy re-loading.

The torpedo men in the fore-ends worked like demons to bring their boat once again to a state of instant readiness. When these sweating ratings leaned panting against the empty racks, Wanklyn was already heading back for the scene of victory and the damaged troopship. He brought *Upholder* to periscope depth for a general look-see. His periscope, about a foot above the Mediterranean, left a feather-trail as he headed towards his obviously crippled target. As he ordered 'Down periscope!' the dawn was just breaking. For some time he pressed on at a depth of 60 feet, until once again he commanded 'Periscope depth – up periscope!' Crouched down on the deck as the periscope left its well, his eyes glued to the eyepiece whilst the vessel's all-seeing eye was still below the sea's surface, all he could momentarily see was water, water everywhere, until the periscope burst suddenly through the surface, and the quickening daylight revealed the details of his previous work.

He could see one troopship and one destroyer standing by: the latter vessel circling the lamed trooper in a protective screen.

'Down periscope!' Wanklyn ordered. At 60 feet *Upholder* pressed on like a hungry shark, the only sound within her being the low purr of her motors.

'Periscope depth – up periscope!' There was the same crouch as he caught the periscope handles, the same glint was in his eyes as surface was broken and the day again glimmered through.

Wanklyn swung the periscope round for an all-embracing view, walking the necessary circle. 'Down periscope!' A few minutes went by. 'Up periscope. Flood Q's: Down periscope!' was now the order.

He could still see the sharp bow of a destroyer streaking towards his periscope. The Engine Room Artificer flooded Q-tanks; *Upholder* dropped like a stone; a threshing, deafening din drowned the hum of the submarine's motors.

The crew hunched their shoulders in fear of the impending attack, which might have been either the crash ramming, or a pattern of depth-charges. That roaring, devastating sound passed inches over them – a long indrawn sigh of relief burst from the crew. The 'depth-charges' never came.

Long minutes went by. Next order: 'Periscope depth – up periscope!' followed. Wanklyn saw the dark sea as the periscope pushed its way surface-wards, the sunlight penetrated the last few feet of water.

Then, as the periscope burst from its under-water world, he gasped, for directly before his eyes was the vast black wall of the damaged troopship's side.

'Down periscope: take her down to 80 feet' he commanded. He was too close to deliver his intended attack.

Upholder's hydroplanes took her down 60 feet; at 80 feet she levelled off. The helmsman steered the same course, on and on towards the trooper's hull, the crew not knowing if 20,000 inert tons would come crashing into them, sending them to the bottom after the first ghastly shock.

More than probably the submariners heard the grind and creak of protesting metal as that dive proceeded. Two thousand yards beyond and *Upholder* swung on her heel into position for an attack.

At 0845: 'Stand by one and two torpedoes!' said the green lights in the fore-ends. 'Periscope depth' said Wanklyn. 'Up periscope.' He followed the eyepiece up from his crouch, as it emerged from its well. His hands grasped the handles until his knuckles whitened; there in perfect position for a devastating attack was the damaged trooper.

'Fire one-fire two,' he rapped. The green lights turned to red in the fore-ends, a second time within a few hours. Twice the *Upholder's* crew felt the slight shudder, twice they felt the air-pressure on their ears, as the torpedoes whooshed forth on their one and only voyage.

Both missiles crashed into the side of the 20,000-ton *Oceania*. She went down in minutes.

Unbeaten's Captain, Lieutenant-Commander Woodward, there to the eastward, goggled in amazement into his own periscope as he saw two great explosions burst open the ship he was himself about to attack. No one but he could describe his emotions, as he saw Fate play its ironical trick, snatching his bird from under his very eyes.

Wanklyn ordered: 'Down periscope.' His immediate work was finished, and well finished. The only sign of emotion observed in this critical moment, by those about him, was the slow thoughtful stroking of his beard. Then he slowly rubbed his large competent hands together.

Upholder entered Malta Harbour on 20 September. The fifteenth patrol was unique in *Upholder's* record: during the whole period at sea not so much as a wisp of enemy smoke was spotted.

It was not until 18 October, a Saturday, that Wanklyn steered out on his sixteenth patrol. His feelings were undoubtedly very mixed as he negotiated the boom. Being a glutton for work, recent barren days had left him hungry for convincing action. He prayed that satisfying targets would loom into his view. Those prayers remained unanswered, for though the following day bred a recrudescence of hope as the periscope framed a suspicious object, it proved to be nothing more promising than the masts of a wreck. And during four ensuing days, the magic eye reflected nothing whatever beyond a waste of sky and sea. Targets appeared to be growing scarce: even one of Britain's topmost submarine aces couldn't spot a single one. Maybe it was due to his own activity, for Captain Simpson said this of David Wanklyn: 'He has an uncanny flair for being in exactly the right places at the right times!' Still the sea continued bare; not to be wondered at, all said and done, for Wanklyn had by this time sunk 104,000 tons of enemy shipping, badly damaged another 10,000 tons and inflicted serious hurt on two formidable cruisers. *Upholder* was somewhat like an enthusiastic game-shot who has destroyed all available birds, and must be content to go empty away from the denuded moor.

But on Friday, the 24th, at 0730, hope renewed itself, as a snap-sight of the funnel and masts of a single ship lifted the load of boredom that the crew felt grow heavier each day. *Upholder* vibrated forcefully as she closed at full speed towards this stranger, but, to the general chagrin, her sides carried the emblem of the Red Cross. Undisturbed, she was allowed to continue her way, and the curtain of boredom began again to descend.

Still, on Saturday at 0935 the sea's monotonous surface was broken by the dark hull of a ship. 'Diving stations' sounded promptly through the submarine. After long waiting an attack was in prospect. Alas for rising hopes! As *Upholder* speeded up and closed in towards the object, all torpedoes at the ready, the lettering on the stranger's sides read PLM20. Nothing more worth while than a French collier!

'Down periscope. Fall out. Diving stations. Break off the attack' was the best Wanklyn could command under the disappointing circumstances. Once more, patrol completed, *Upholder* entered Malta Harbour with her torpedo tubes and racks still complete. Not a single tinfish had been expended; there were no bars to be added to the jolly Roger.

CHAPTER 11

A VICTORIOUS WEEK-END

FRIDAY, 7 November, saw H.M. submarine *Upholder* with her hatches clipped shut and her scanty crew rigid at harbour stations. Tiny she was, lean as a rake, as potential a source of danger to the enemy as any line-of-battle ship. Her present departure differed in no way from the many previous excursions. By now *Upholder's* fame was well established.

All the 'Good lucks', the 'Good huntings', the 'Happy returns', had been shouted, hands had been wrung, the thick-ended jests had been exchanged.

With the propeller-wash making the only noise, she slipped through the boom defence, which closed silently behind her, and the tiny steel hull and its thirty-four occupants merged into the darkening twilight.

Trim dive completed, she pressed on towards her patrol area. In that gathering gloom her shape was now only visible to eyes with the seeing capacity of an owl's; and stealthily she continued on the surface until, at half-past-eleven that same evening, a prowling aircraft dropped a flare. As it floated down its unearthly brilliance lit up the submarine's lean hull, disclosing her as clearly as if a midsummer sun illuminated her; and obviously keen eyes were spotting her every movement from on high.

The klaxon horn brayed thrice. Officer of the Watch and bridge lookouts tumbled like acrobats down the conning tower; already *Upholder's* bows were dipping down and water was drowning her casing. There was no time for precedence or ceremony; get down and get down as quickly as hell was the only thought: As sure as sin a pattern of bombs would follow the revealing flare: it was an airman's dream come true.

The upper hatch was clipped, and to watchful eyes the depth-gauge seemed to stick fast at 10 feet only. A sitting shot, of course – only a beginner at the job could miss this chance. No, the gauge registered 30 feet, then 50 feet then – glory be! 80 feet. She literally tumbled under in eagerness to gain the shelter of a watery cushion. But she took cover for only a brief ten minutes or so. At the end of the ten minutes' submersion, the dripping fabric broke surface again, for Wanklyn was in a hurry to be up and doing, and chance the luck. Aircraft hadn't the same deadly potentiality as destroyers and escort craft, which could pursue remorselessly, with apparently unlimited supplies of high explosives to make life unpleasant for such as occupied their business under great waters. Evidently the aircraft had given up the business as a bad job, for there was no disturbance. Just before dawn on the next morning, around 0400 'Diving stations' resounded through the cramped interior of the submarine, for Petty Officer Swainston had seen a darker shadow in the darkness.

By then David Wanklyn was already on the bridge, having shot up from below like a cork from a pop-gun. The vessel was speeded up. Her Commander ordered: 'Stand by all tubes' as he sought hard for any sign of the identity of what was merely a distant shadow. It was something a little out of the ordinary, obviously: here was no surface craft, its humped silhouette gave the lie to such a theory.

'It's a U-boat-Perla class!' The almost incredible announcement flashed through the tensed interior, and all hearing it nodded satisfaction. Here was even combat – submarine *versus* submarine. A U-boat was the potential killer of uncounted tons of invaluable shipping – and there was more than a little British tonnage afloat in the vicinity.

The torpedo-room was at the ready. The control-room helmsman listened intently for any change of course; the E.R.A. and his attendant stokers nursed their engines as tenderly as any affectionate mother, just as the L.T.O.'s did their motors. It was everyone's attack and every member of the crew of *Upholder* was proud to bear part and lot in it. Which would first open fire: the enemy U-boat or the *Upholder's* skipper?

Any second could bring an enemy torpedo tearing through the flimsy skin of *Upholder*. Both contestants had about the same armament, with the odds slightly in favour of the U-boat as she probably carried a larger outfit of torpedoes.

There was no doubt about this one. This was no British T-class submarine. This was an enemy.

There were long-drawn-out minutes of suspense as *Upholder* moved in. Was the Italian making similar dispositions? Was she working around to get *Upholder* in her sights?

At ten minutes past four Wanklyn decided to dive and fire from periscope depth. The risk of being spotted on the surface was too great.

He signalled: 'Up periscope.' There was the other sub. perfectly in his sights. Range? Slightly under 1,500 yards. In orderly sequence four torpedoes left *Upholder's* tubes. A small fortune in money but worth it.

Wanklyn kept his periscope raised and watched the other sub. narrowly. He saw, too, the four filmy tracks as the torpedoes sped on their way.

Then crash! He saw a towering column of water grow alongside the shadowy enemy sub., followed by a lurid purple red flash.

Seconds later – it seemed like an eternity – they all heard the dull thump, the sound of an explosion travelling through the water.

The stricken submarine rolled and twisted like a dying whale and in a few minutes disappeared from sight. An enemy submarine killed less than twelve hours after beginning patrol.

Gone were memories of the recent blank patrols. Thoughts of 'hoodoo' disappeared like a flash.

Wanklyn surfaced and carried out a comprehensive search of the oil-fouled water.

There was nothing remotely resembling a human being among the evil-smelling scum on the surface. The first streaks of dawn were showing when *Upholder* dived and proceeded on patrol with a general re-loading of tubes to occupy some of their time.

For a while Wanklyn played tag with some aircraft - a seaplane and a couple of heavy bombers. Finally he slipped down to 80 feet. There was no point in running unnecessary risks.

Around this time *Upholder's* radio operator had deciphered an important signal stating that a British surface force would be passing through this area on the night of the 8th. An important point to remember for two reasons.

Firstly it would be unfortunate if *Upholder* had sighted that force and had fired a salvo into it while under the impression that it was an enemy squadron.

Secondly had such a thing happened he would have been hunted by the screening destroyers.

Shortly after twilight *Upholder* surfaced and began the usual routine. The air inside the sub. was freshened and the diesels worked double speed charging up the batteries while the air compressors did a similar duty for the air-groups.

It was a few minutes before midnight when a sharpeyed look-out reported: 'Objects bearing 240 degrees.' Wanklyn studied it.

'It's Force K,' he remarked. The British force. Wanklyn decided to dive to 80 feet until Force K had passed on its way.

The crew heard the increasing clamour of the screws as the ships passed near or overhead and smiled a little grimly. Would Force K have been steaming over them in orderly array if they had not sunk that enemy U-boat?

Force K's allotted task was to attack a large enemy convoy carrying men and supplies to North Africa. There is little doubt that the U-boat was posted where it was to meet such an attacking force. *Upholder* surfaced. Wanklyn and his crew had their just reward.

Shortly after one o'clock they heard terrific gunfire ahead. *Upholder* closed in a little to watch the fun. Wanklyn saw from his bridge a sight granted to few submarine commanders.

Force K had met up with the convoy and its escort and was setting about it in workmanlike fashion. Wanklyn counted five motor vessels and one tanker blazing furiously. The sea around them was an inferno of flame, throwing towering columns of reddened smoke to the sky. Even as he watched he saw another ship blow up with a tremendous explosion.

Finally the surface ships completed their task leaving behind them only destruction. Yet another convoy would not reach Rommel.

Force K, consisting of H.M.S. *Penelope*, popularly known in the Mediterranean as H.M.S. *Pepper Pot* (and made famous by C. S. Forester in his story, *The Ship*) the *Aurora*, two light cruisers, and the destroyers *Lively* and *Lance*.

Soon only *Upholder* and the ruins of the convoy remained so far as Wanklyn could tell. He closed in to the chaotic scene and saw destroyers weaving in and out among the blazing hulks. Their outlines assumed queer shapes as the flames were reflected from their gleaming sides. He decided that possibly it was *Lively* and *Lance* so he dived, but only to periscope depth.

At first dawn he lifted periscope and finally identified the mystery shapes as three single-funnelled Italian destroyers of Aviere class. He stalked them carefully then dead ahead he saw one stopped. Right in his sights!

For once he was hunting destroyers instead of them hunting him.

'Fire one.' *Upholder* shivered slightly and lifted a fraction as the weight left her bow then settled snugly down again. Wanklyn saw the bubbling trail and heard the asdic rating report: 'Torpedo running, sir.'

Now it meant waiting. It was a hit. Maybe not a total kill but one enemy destroyer was certainly out of commission for a long time.

Wanklyn scouted around cautiously and on one of his surveys he saw the destroyer he had hit low in the water. Another destroyer was standing by her. It was a temptation. He had three torpedoes left. One more for the already stricken ship and the other two for the second destroyer would show a fair dividend.

Wanklyn resisted the temptation. He reasoned that after the catastrophic destruction of the convoy something larger would almost certainly show up and he held his hand.

Something did turn up. To *Upholder's* crew it seemed that half the available Italian air force filled the sky. Theirs must have been a depressing picture. The shattered remnants of the convoy – those which still remained above the surface were still burning furiously.

In the centre was a destroyer, almost bow under, stern cocked up in the air. A cripple.

Upholder judiciously slipped below. A terrific explosion shook the submarine and conjectures ranged from a new and secret weapon against submarines to one of the last transports giving up the ghost in a spectacular blast.

It was in fact one of the motor ships shattered by a final upheaval. As it happened close to the damaged destroyer her crew undoubtedly took a bleak view of life as it presented itself to them at the moment.

The scorching blast as the motor ship blew up was the least of their problems. Somewhere in the vicinity was a British submarine prowling around, no doubt, sparring for an opening in which to deliver the coup de grace. A depressing morning indeed, viewed from an Italian aspect.

Wanklyn's decision to wait for bigger game was justified. He risked being spotted by one of the numerous aircraft flying around like swifts on a summer evening and lifted his periscope.

There, framed beautifully in the mirror, and obligingly drawing closer were two cruisers and four destroyers. At the moment they were pushing along a gleaming bow wave which spelled speed and plenty of it but on their present course they would soon reach the scene of devastation and would possibly slow down.

The news filtered through *Upholder* and her hull was scarcely wide enough to cope with the smiles. This was a submariners' dream come true, but for the one flaw. She was short of torpedoes. Even one more would have made it perfection.

By this time the damaged destroyer was being slowly towed away, but she would not be entirely forgotten. First things first.

All unnecessary lights had been switched off and in the half-light inside the submarine it looked like some diabolical setting conceived by Heath Robinson with a touch of Dante. There were shining pipes, valves, wheel gauges, casting back pin-point reflections of light with the half-naked men standing immobile except for the minimum degree of movement imposed by their task. Their bodies too, gleamed with sweat.

A last quick peep showed Wanklyn that the two cruisers had a screen of destroyers on either beam with two more zigzagging like drunken seamen astern.

The detector screen around those cruisers was almost 100 per cent. The destroyers on the beams would be probing from right ahead to well astern on either side and the two zigzagging ships behind would be carrying out a fan of listening.

Wanklyn estimated that he had seven or eight minutes in which to make his attack.

And in seven minutes' time he considered that the situation was as near perfect as he could expect.

'Fire one, fire two, fire three.'

Wanklyn committed everything to this one salvo. The first torpedo skimmed bare feet ahead of the nearer cruiser, but was not entirely wasted. It blew the bows of the attendant destroyer on the far side.

The second torpedo went raving, crazy mad. Instead of heading straight for the target it started tearing around in delirious circles.

And in a segment of one of those circles lay *Upholder*. To be hit by one of her faulty torpedoes would be the cruellest of fates. The asdic rating could pick up the whistling scream of it as it raced around and with very little imagination the crew convinced themselves that they, too, could hear it.

Finally it swung away and disappeared.

The third torpedo also missed the cruiser by the proverbial coat of grease, but that too, was not entirely thrown away. The screening destroyer on the far side had stopped when the first 'kipper' blew off her bow. She got the second one, reared up, started a climbing twisting roll and simply slid beneath the surface as if a vast hole had opened up and she had fallen into it.

For *Upholder*, now bare of torpedoes, to remain in the vicinity would be foolhardy. Wanklyn turned her head towards Malta and put a few miles between himself and the scene of desolation and misery behind him.

It was a day to remember.

One task remained, and that carried a risk. Wanklyn surfaced when he was a few miles away, fixed his position and signalled a résumé of the day's activities. No doubt others might be ordered to be on-stage for the finale both in the air and under the water.

And *Upholder* went on her way rejoicing. It had been quite a week-end at sea. One U-boat and one destroyer sunk beyond dispute and another destroyer damaged so badly that her survival was problematical.

Careful fingers sewed over her Jolly Roger as she approached Malta and when she entered there were three new bars on it, one of them with a large letter U in its centre fluttering bravely as she moored.

Upholder had been at sea only eighty-seven hours on that patrol, a patrol which has been handed down as a legend: a record.

CHAPTER 12

ATTACK BY ASDIC

ON Tuesday, 25 November, H.M. submarine *Upholder* left Malta Harbour on her eighteenth patrol. She had her usual crew aboard, and each man was imbued with the same fighting spirit as had animated him from the beginning of the commission, plus a complete and almost mystical confidence in the Commander. This was a happy, successful boat, with a dazzling record of success that her few setbacks could in no way diminish.

By Thursday morning the submarine was off the Calabrian coast, down there near the 'toe' of Italy, which promised to be a fertile hunting-ground. The first flush of a new dawn tinged the fleecy clouds overhead with a delicate pink and she dived alertly, since there were awkward waters to patrol, with every prospect of the full rigours of war bursting on her before the sun rose. By 0715 two-thirds of the crew were having the sparse breakfast that a shortage of stores compelled. They did not alter their routine as did most submarine crews, who changed the programme fully about, so that meals were served by night, when they could be eaten in a fresher atmosphere. Very probably the idea possessing them was that their scanty rations did not justify any substantial change in the order of feeding.

The breakfasters' mouths were still full of food when: 'Diving stations! One tanker, two destroyers up top' sounded through the compartments. Here, apparently, was Wanklyn. Luck again: enemy in sight within forty-eight hours of leaving port. At 0739 David Wanklyn closed in and ordered: 'Start the attack. Stand by all tubes!'

'This looks like it again,' said a couple of ratings for'ard.

Upholder closed her distance steadily, unhurriedly. The surface craft were zigzagging vigorously, doing their best to disconcert any likely attack. A submarine is usually given only one real chance per convoy; it is incumbent on her to hit with her first salvo, and this type of assault differs considerably from that of one by gunfire, where several rounds can be fired before finding the deadly range. Torpedo-tracks are revealing and invite immediate and deadly counter-attack.

Wanklyn's periscope bubbled a foamy track astern as the submarine beneath it headed towards the promising target. 'Fire one, fire two, fire three, fire four!' said the Commander precisely. Four times that uncanny shudder shook the little boat, but the gods of chance were not smiling on British valour that morning off Cape Spartivento, and Wanklyn was unable to claim decisive hits. The enemy vessels proceeded without undue concern, most probably unaware that any attack had been launched. Any amount of reasons could be advanced for this failure: conceivably the torpedoes themselves were faulty, or the ships zigzagged at precisely the right moment-as occasionally happens. No one can account for the fact, but those Italians were lucky men that day.

Having lost at least half her teeth, *Upholder* chugged lazily along on the surface on 1 December – a Monday. The bridge look-outs, everlastingly alert, suddenly spotted eight dark shadows heading directly towards the submarine. The time was 0437, and it was very dark.

The old familiar command echoed through the hull: 'Diving stations. Stand by all tubes.' David Wanklyn strained his exceptionally keen eyes until they made out the shadows: three cruisers and five destroyers. The tension on the bridge communicated itself by an invisible grapevine throughout the submarine. The pygmy and the giant all over again! Wanklyn knew well enough that he was going to be spotted before he could launch his attack: the enemy weren't fools, and their scientific equipment was improving with each week that passed.

'All down below,' he ordered. 'Dive, dive, dive.' He was, as usual, last to leave the bridge. *Upholder* was submerging quickly, her surface speed giving her an extra push. The conning-tower hatch was shut and clipped, and the periscope was being raised in a few seconds. Through that periscope Wanklyn could see nothing. By surfacing again he would certainly be spotted immediately. His only hope – a slender one – was to fire by asdic bearings, where the odds were against success.

'Seventy feet' he instructed, and the submarine planed down to the exact required depth. The asdic rating reported the bearings of the enemy flotilla. The First Lieutenant notified position: 'Submarine at 70 feet, Sir.' It was eerie in the damp control-room: the clock ticked its seconds away methodically, and each tick was repeated by a quickened heartbeat. The time went by until 0500. An up-to-the-minute attack guided by pure science was about to take place. The asdic rating continued to report the changing positions of the cruiser force. The depth-gauge needle was steady as a rock on the 70 feet mark. The planesmen, backs to the control-room, swung their hydroplane-control wheels around slightly. 'Hope the skipper hits the bull!' said someone in the engine-room, denied much knowledge of events, but infected by the prevailing tension. One and all were breathing prayers for Wanklyn – even if some erred on the side of near-blasphemy. For the submariner's faith in his individual skipper is something that has to be experienced to be believed.

The clock now registered three minutes past five. Suspense still hung like an impalpable smoke-screen in the bowels of the *Upholder*; and the tick-tick of that clock sounded unnaturally loud in the general hush. Three minutes and thirty seconds past five! A report came from the asdic rating: the big hand of the clock was coming up to four minutes past 5 a.m. Wanklyn's lips pursed into an expression of determination. 'Fire one, fire two, fire three, fire four!' he said crisply. The boat bounced a little more than usual, as though sterner determination than ever propelled the missiles.

'All torpedoes running,' announced the asdic-specialist. Wanklyn's big hand caressed the side of his expressive beard.

'Torpedoes gone clean under the target!' came in a sickened gulp from the asdic-man.

They had missed completely: four valuable rounds expended in vain! And, as before, the surface knew nothing of the attack, but went serenely on their way. Of all the luck! It certainly seemed as if a serial hoodoo had settled on the *Upholder*, which blew her main ballast tanks and surfaced fifty minutes later, remained surfaced for a while, and then dived and laid course for the recently left Base.

Wanklyn's attitude towards his craft was that of a scientist, one who studies absorbedly every element to analyse its significance and its potentialities. He was absorbed in probing into the cause of that discomfiting failure. His final conclusion was that the torpedoes simply

SUBMARINE UPHOLDER

hadn't had time to gain their required depth. But now the *Upholder's* teeth were drawn, unless some trivial chance occurred to use her gun. Such a vague hope proved fruitless, however, and her patrol ended on 3 December.

The submarine's nineteenth patrol, lasting from 12 to 21 December, resulted in no offensive attacks on her part, consequently she had no successes to report. Most of the time she was hunted rather than being a hunter, and the experiences she underwent were worse than when she was pressing the attack. Off Cape Spartivento she was pestered continuously by air activity, by anti-submarine trawlers and E-boats, which maintained unbroken control of her working area during the entire time she occupied it. Her previous successful activities had unquestionably put the wind up the enemy, and she was outlawed by everything that could be brought into action. Taken by and large it was a nerve-racking experience: frustrating to men whose desire was to kill, rather than to be killed. Just what the enemy expended on high explosives in the long attempt to exterminate the *Upholder* is not on record, but it must have been phenomenal. To her crew a new return to port was as welcome as the near approach of Christmas, though a Malta Christmas promised to be anything but a season of plenty and goodwill!

So the year 1941 was drawing to a close. A year which had at its commencement seen *Upholder* as a virgin submarine, was ending with the submarine's reputation almost a legend.

It is no exaggeration to say that H.M. submarine *Upholder* was the ace of Britain's under-water Navy. One year's intelligent activity by her devoted crew had resulted in the definite sinking of fifteen ships, five more severely damaged, even in all probability sunk or rendered useless; of these trophies five were naval craft: formidable antagonists. In one single brief patrol Wanklyn's submarine had destroyed 40,000 tons of shipping that must have been invaluable to the enemy; the loss of combatant forces resulting therefrom can never be accurately estimated. It was an incredible year for such a comparatively trivial fighting unit to look back upon. Taken by and large, 1941 was a remarkable twelve months for the Submarine Service as a whole.

That year had but two days to run before its final leaf was ripped from the calendar. Christmas, for the *Upholders* was merely a memory, with a lingering hangover, perhaps – entirely justifiable, considering the rigours endured!

On 29 December the submarine left harbour for a single day's peaceful exercise. Peaceful? Merely a practice business: a dummy run in naval language. For the only time thus far in leaving port, the bearded figure of David Wanklyn was not in sight on the bridge. He was in the official phrase: 'Resting ashore' – and no man deserved a spell of leisure more than he. Lieutenant G. P. Norman deputised for him there on *Upholder's* bridge, and in the event proved his worthiness to be one of Wanklyn's band of brothers.

In full clear view of the island's shore the exercises were successfully carried out, without much excitement, and at the completion, course was set for the boom defence. Even in these friendly waters the bridge lookouts maintained their vigilance, since even though the waters were well swept, there was always a danger of attack from the sky. Malta was not well provided with air defence, owing to the difficulties of transport, both of men, material and fuel.

The half-expected attack came that same afternoon of the 29th, and it came from overhead. Messerschmitt fighter planes came streaking down out of the dingy blue of a December sky towards the submarine, their cannon blazing fury as heralds of total destruction. The pilots were out for a kill: grimly determined to wipe *Upholder* from the Navy List. To their mind she was a sitting target, her destruction inevitable,

'Dive, dive, dive!' Norman yelled. 'Ahooa-ahooa-ahooa!' blared the klaxon to back up his warning. Action followed alert with commendable speed. The main vents opened. The planesmen in a split second manned their hydroplane wheels. A whistling scream of air howled from fore and aft on both sides of the submarine as the air was forced out of the ballast tanks.

Her bows were dipping under, her look-outs were scrambling like electrified imps down the conning tower; the cannon shells from the hostile planes were creating miniature waterspouts astern of the diving vessel. All hell appeared to be let loose. In a trice the conning tower was submerging, the last look-out was down the hatch.

The temporary Commanding Officer was on the top rung of the conning-tower ladder, and the water swirled furiously around what little of *Upholder* still showed on the surface. Those vicious cannon-made waterspouts were everywhere around the swirls. They were registering hits on the conning tower, and shrapnel flew like hail from the cowl. A fragment hit Norman at the back of the skull. Another fragment, or it may have been a bullet, went through his right arm; a large number of splinters smashed into his body. He fell from the ladder to the conning-tower's lower hatch, shocked, bleeding badly. And the sea was inexorably climbing up the sides of that conning tower. The hatch above was still open.

Upholder was diving fast; it was only a matter of split seconds before the conning tower was smothered, and with that happening, water would come cascading down the open hatch like a miniature Niagara. Disaster was imminent – life hung on a thread – but that thread was a strong one: its name was Norman. Wounded and shocked as he was, he retained his presence of mind, and estimated the risks – and the hopes. He acted in the best traditions of the Submarine Service. Losing blood fast, suffering intense pain, he rallied enough to climb that vertical ladder once again, to draw down the vital hatch and clip it securely shut. An instant more and the *Upholder* was completely submerged – and but for Norman it would have been her final dive. As it was, disaster had been averted by the breadth of a hair, and Norman's courageous act had saved H.M. submarine *Upholder* – saved her as an instrument of David Wanklyn's further successes.

CHAPTER 13

NEW YEAR'S EVE DISASTER

IT was 7 p.m. on New Year's Eve, 1941: a time when even the much-harassed people of Malta were making preparations for the seasonal celebrations; summoning their friends to join them in merrymaking and in praying that 1942 might bring a cessation to the purgatory they were enduring. War could not suspend all normal human activities; death abounded, certainly, but life went on.

Without doubt, the *Upholders* felt twinges of sadness on this last night of the Old Year, if only for the fact that their New Year's Eve was to be spent at sea, where roistering celebrations were out of the question. No popping of champagne corks or blowing froth off pints of beer for the brethren of the underseas.

More than probably David Wanklyn himself felt a touch of homesickness on this occasion. Although no Scot, he had a love for Scotland and the pleasures that country afforded. And, as everybody knows, Hogmanay is the night of nights across the Border, when the stolid Northerners really let things go with a bang and a splash! But Wanklyn did not allow nostalgic sentiment to interfere with the business ahead, and his voice was as steady and practical as usual as he ordered 'Slow ahead, both,' on that evening at 7 p.m. Festival or no festival, the boom opened to give exit to the *Upholder*, which sailed purposefully through to open water and vanished into the darkness. Modern war doesn't allow interludes for fun and games to any noticeable extent: it's a twenty-four hours a day job, a 365 days a year task with only occasional intermissions when man and machine must both be rested lest sheer exhaustion defeats their purpose. Wanklyn hoped, but did not know, that 1942's dawning was to bring him an outstanding triumph.

By 2107 that New Year's Eve, all conjecture about the future was wiped out of the crew's minds by the braying of the klaxon. The submarine was plunging swiftly to the deeps, seeking escape from plummeting, avenging aircraft. Twelve minutes later, the immediate scare being ended, she surfaced again and surged purposefully forward towards her appointed patrol area. The rest of the night passed uneventfully, with only the throb of her diesels and muttered helm orders to break the stark silence of the Mediterranean waters. The watches changed at midnight; those who remembered the occasion wished each other the compliments of the season – what kind of a season they naturally wondered! At all events, they had seen the change-over of the years on the surface, in clean air, and not in a stifling metal can of a ship. This comparative freedom allowed them to turn their thoughts homewards. Britain was being blasted by heavy bombing. And those they loved were in Britain. It was twelve months – nineteen patrols ago – since they had seen them. Letters were scarcer than wild mushrooms at Christmas-time. The shortage of food in Malta they could accept, reserving to themselves the inalienable right of a matlow, especially a submariner, to moan and grouse.

But shortage of mail, lack of news, was something of a different calibre. Did silence mean … ? Was there nobody left alive to write at home … ? Was that home a smoking heap of rubble, with rescue parties of haggard-eyed men searching … ?

They could endure, to a point, the far too frequent depth-charging at sea, the almost constant strain of action stations, and the bombing ashore. All of that they could endure because they knew they were hitting back, and hitting back hard.

At times it seemed that the 10th Submarine Flotilla was fighting alone against the combined might of the Axis navies in the Mediterranean.

It was a mixed bag of thoughts with which to herald the dawning New Year of 1942. Would their luck hold? Was the Old Man – David Wanklyri – such a favourite of the Gods?

Upholder signalised the dawn of 1942 by diving at 0700 and staying down. Her crew were suffering from no New Year's Eve hang-over; no opportunity had occurred to earn one! There seemed to be a great deal of air activity; bombers were overhead constantly, and it would appear that some movement of transports was meditated. Wanklyn rubbed those oversized hands of his together and – waited. Inevitably something would happen. *Upholder* attracted trouble as a jam-boiling attracts wasps.

At 1600 her periscope sight revealed Agrigento in the distance. Normal submerged routine went on. The second day of the new year dawned, with no outstanding event recorded in the log. Bombers over Trapani were spotted. Trapani is on the extreme west coast of Sicily, somewhat north of Marsala, where Horatio Nelson used to buy wine for his cabin stores. But there was no rich Marsala in *Upholder's* wine-lockers, and the only promise of celebration was when on 4 January a 5,000-ton tanker was spotted in the darkness. This gave an opportunity for letting go a display of submarine fireworks in the shape of a couple of damaged torpedoes.

One of these misguided missiles promptly flopped to the bottom where it exploded practically under the submarine, giving *Upholder* as bad a shake-up as any enemy depth-charge had managed to do. However, despite this mishap, two more torpedoes were fired at the tanker, one of them registering a hit, but did no more than inflict damage without sending her to the bottom. In an attempt to complete the task, *Upholder* surfaced and engaged the victim with her pitifully inadequate 12-pounder deck-gun. Whereupon the damaged Italian proceeded to open up a fast and furious defence with her two Breda guns. These maintained an accurate and galling fire and compelled Wanklyn to break off the engagement, since his armament was no match for that carried by the enemy.

But by 0500 on 5 January the British submarine was still on the surface. Dawn was still some time away; Wanklyn had one torpedo left, and only one. Bad luck had dogged this patrol, in spite of *Upholder* having damaged one important ship.

Five-thirty came and there wasn't much time left before diving. Tension grew, the look-outs on their toes strained their eyes to aching-point to pierce the gloom that enveloped the Mediterranean in that darkest hour before the dawn. The black seas that listlessly slapped *Upholder's* lean sides gave the impression that she was afloat in a bottomless pit. Wanklyn got himself to the bridge in readiness for the first break of day; as he did so a look-out bawled: 'Object bearing 180 degrees.' That was dead astern. The cry brought Wanklyn's quickly focused night-glasses into play and disclosed a dark, not clearly distinguishable something approaching rapidly.

'She looks like an anti-submarine trawler,' diagnosed the Commander, to whom all silhouettes of surface craft were as familiar as his own reflection in a mirror. 'All below! Dive, dive, dive!' He, pressed the diving hooter button three times and the weird 'Ahooa-ahooa-ahooa' screamed through the submarine's interior. A hardened submariner can and often does sleep through loud explosions outboard, but it is an open bet that no one ever slept through the scream of the diving klaxon! That unearthly din simply lifts the hair straight on end with its urgent demand.

The boat was manned for diving; her bows were dipping down within seconds from the moment when Wanklyn pressed the button. The casing was awash as he closed and clipped the conning-tower hatch. His tall figure dropped into the control-room hurriedly once he was satisfied that all was secure above; and there were witnesses to swear he practically touched no rung of the vertical ladder in his gymnastic descent.

'Up periscope!' He followed it up in its ascent, and the moment the wash subsided – at 0534 – exclaimed for all within distance to hear: 'A U-boat. Stand by one torpedo.' The preliminaries to attack started forthwith. Continuing his commentary Wanklyn said: 'He's a big fellow – 1,500 tons at least. He's got two guns, and is zigzagging, too!'

It looked as if that extra sense with which David Wanklyn was unquestionably endowed had caused him to dive his submarine in the very nick of time; as well that this was so, for the enemy submarine had spotted *Upholder* first.

He had to get his attack commenced with the utmost speed. The enemy big fellow could have dived at any moment. She was less than 1,000 yards away when,, grasping the periscope handles until his knuckles whitened, he rasped 'Fire!'

There was only one shot to be fired and it had to be a good one. The time was 0539 when the torpedo catapulted from its tube with the usual shivering accompaniments. Wanklyn watched its tracks through his still-raised periscope. He hadn't long to wait: a mere thirty-five seconds only. That was quite sufficient suspense.

'Brump!' That forlorn hope of a missile hit the enemy vessel immediately for'ard of the foremost gun. An incredible waterspout shot skywards; vast volumes of flame surrounded the area. It might have been an outsize Fifth of November rather than 5 January; here was a veritable Brock's benefit of a show. The entire sea appeared to be aflame, but through the holocaust Wanklyn saw the target dip and disappear.

She broke up under his eyes; thirty seconds more and the gratified crew could hear the twisting and cracking of tortured metal as the unfortunate boat crumpled into hissing scrap. The seas quenched the flames over the area of combat.

By 0546 *Upholder* was at 28 feet in almost the precise spot where her now mangled victim had been.

'Stand by to surface!' came the crisp command. 'Surface!' equally crisply followed. *Upholder* rose rapidly from her water coverage; as rapidly skipper and lookouts manned the dripping bridge – dripping with oil on this occasion, for the greasy film that had escaped from the doomed enemy sub. had not burned. Wanklyn was looking for any sign of life in that grisly sea. Sharp cries from the look-outs indicated that the quest was not in vain. Three heads were bobbing about in the scum.

'Call up extra hands from the control-room,' he ordered. And on their arrival, he instructed them to climb out on the casing and collect the survivors, alive or dead.

With the help of their erstwhile antagonists, enmity having died with victory, the first two contrived to scramble aboard *Upholder*, aided by the quickly thrown ropes; the third was dragged aboard, only to collapse on the superstructure, more dead than alive., The first two were able to climb down the conning-tower ladder. They were saved: just oil-soaked non-combatants for the rest of the war.

The third survivor was still unconscious on *Upholder's* casing. To get a limp, unconscious human body down the conning tower of a small, 630-ton submarine is no child's play. The quickest, and presumably the safest way of dealing with the emergency would have been to heave the unconscious fragment of humanity back into the sea. *Upholder* was in extremely dangerous waters, and her own safety had of necessity to be a prime consideration. Any moment might bring a lightning attack from the air, for without doubt that display of leaping flame must have been spotted by someone.

But humanity prevailed: a rope was used to drag the inanimate figure to the bridge, after which it was lowered gently down the conning-tower hatch. As the Italian was half-way down the trunking the rope became jammed in the casing. At that identical moment hydrophone effects from revolving propellers were reported by the asdic rating, and notwithstanding frantic efforts the rope continued jammed. Under the circumstances it was impossible for *Upholder* to dive into the security of deep waters; the strained rope over the hatch-coaming wouldn't permit the hatch to be shut. (This was a trick that British boarding parties on U-boats employed, except that they used a chain instead of a rope.) So it looked as if one insignificant Italian, unconscious though he might be, could lose for Britain her most famous submarine, for the hydrophone effect still continued and the obstinate rope was still hopelessly jammed.

To an accompaniment of real lower-deck curses, it was ultimately cleared. The Italian, still unconscious, was by now lying inert on the control-room deck. There was a quick scamper down the conning tower by the rescue party and the look-outs, and at 0601 H.M. submarine *Upholder* plunged deeply, after being surfaced for a period of fifteen minutes.

Submerged, she proceeded resolutely on course to Base. The three survivors were given exemplary treatment: dry clothes and hot drinks being willingly provided. Once these unfortunates got their second wind, Wanklyn questioned them and found them fairly willing to talk. They admitted to being from the Italian submarine *Ammiraglio St. Bon*, of 1,500 tons, at least two and a half times the size of the victorious Britisher. They revealed how they had spotted *Upholder* before being discerned, and had actually closed the breech of their for'ard gun as our submarine dived. They went on to say that they were on passage from Messina to Palermo for repairs.

These lucky survivors were: Lieutenant Como, whose home was in Pola. He was aged twenty-four, with only six months' service in submarines to his credit. He mentioned that he had visited Plymouth in 1938.

Valentino Chico was a Petty Officer Telegraphist, aged twenty-one. He was a Sicilian, and, like Como, had no more than six months' submarine service to his credit. The third of this rescued trio was Ernest Fiore: a veteran of thirty, hailing from Reggio, that neat little port up Italy's west coast. A bachelor, he had entered the Italian Navy in 1929, had served until 1933; after a lapse he was recalled for service in 1935. Once again he was summoned to the colours in 1936, and then, again, finally, in 1939. Fiore was by trade a bricklayer, and extremely anxious to return to his normal vocation.

Since Fiore was inclined to be communicative, he admitted that the *Ammiraglio St. Bon* had carried no German officers; the run-of-the-mill ratings had scant liking for that arrogant breed. Indeed they hadn't much time for their own national overlords. The main reason for this lack of admiring comradeship was the fact that Italian officers showed no consideration for their crews – a common enough complaint, and one that probably accounted for the ultimate surrender of Mussolini's naval forces. One interesting fact emerged from this cross-examination: on long patrols, only the officers were allowed to wash!

During her return to Malta, enemy planes caused *Upholder* to plunge deep many times, but she made safe port on Thursday, the eighth day of January, with her success flag flying high – fifteen white bars on the black bunting, two more bars with a proud U in their centre, denoting two U-boat sinkings; the total tonnage of shipping destroyed to her credit greater by far than any other British submarine. Here, then, was the ace returning, and of all aboard, the likelihood is that the three Italians were by far the happiest. For them the war was over, and admittedly their escape from ugly death was little short of miraculous but their salvation had been the millionth chance.

Thus David Wanklyn let in the New Year at sea, and, in addition to saving three human lives, had undoubtedly saved innumerable British merchant seamen by putting the *St. Bon* to sleep for ever. Indeed it is conceivable that he saved a considerable amount of our warship tonnage from total destruction. 1942 hadn't made such a bad start, after all!

CHAPTER 14

OFF SICILY

HERE was no suggestion of yawning boredom about the crew of *Upholder* as she negotiated the boom at Malta on the evening of 14 January. Time was 1820, conditions appeared favourable. The business in hand was growing very familiar, but there was no contempt associated with it. One might have thought that, after twenty patrols, the keen zest animating these men would have lessened, but David Wanklyn was an enthusiast and even the dreariest grouser – not that there were any aboard the *Upholder* – could not fail to share his keenness. There had been only a six-day stretch in port, and that could hardly have been described as a rest, since interior work was carried on indefatigably. It says much for a commanding officer's capability that life in *Upholder* offered few dull moments. Wanklyn never waited for adventure to seek him out: he went on the hunt from the moment he started a patrol until, duty completed, he turned his bow homewards.

Not until the trim dive was satisfactorily completed did Wanklyn communicate the area of the coming patrol. Their destination, it appeared, was the entrance to the Gulf of Taranto, and *Upholder* was to be one of a trio of submarines whose ordered duty was to guard that exit from enemy country at all costs, in case a powerful surface force made a sortie on a very important British convoy, heading for sorely harassed Malta. Ten miles to one side of Wanklyn's boat the British submarine *Una* kept station; ten miles to the other the *Torbay* held the flank. With average luck this combination might give the enemy a lot to think about.

Break of day on the 16th saw *Upholder* occupying the centre position of the guard line. The periscopes of all three maintained a close and

119

constant observation across the Gulf, but all that *Upholder* herself sighted was one hospital ship, and later, one merchant vessel, the latter escorted by one destroyer. This modest convoy was too far distant and steaming too rapidly for attack. The expected naval forces were not seen, and so *Upholder* returned to Malta on 23 January as dawn was tingeing the sky with pink.

About this time, Wanklyn refused to be sent home to England, even though the strain imposed on him by constant activity and planning was becoming pretty obvious. He was working himself unmercifully, and the tiredness evident in his face was such that Captain Simpson instructed him to stand off for one patrol, at least. A serious crack-up would have robbed the Submarine Service of its brightest star. Nothing could be more disastrous to a service limited in numbers than the catastrophe likely to follow a breakdown on the part of the senior officer aboard. But though the human element might be spared, at a pinch, the boat herself had necessarily to be kept active, such was the shortage of combatant submarines. Consequently, as *Upholder* sailed through the boom on the evening of 1 February on her twenty-second patrol, the figure of Lieutenant G. P. Norman was on her bridge: that same gallant officer who had been wounded on that identical bridge only a short while before, when the air-attack developed which almost put paid to *Upholder*.

David Wanklyn watched his old command vanish into the obscurity with mixed feelings. Aboard she carried a passenger: Lieutenant Ruble of the U.S. Navy.

It was decreed that Norman's cruising area should be between Marettimo and Palermo on Sicily's north coast. Just after midnight on 2 February, the submarine then being surfaced, it was found advisable to reduce speed, as very heavy head seas were battering hard at the small vessel, gushing up her sides and over the conning tower; cascades of spray deluged the look-outs and actually penetrated down the hatch to the control-room. She still remained surfaced, however, until revealing dawn threatened her, when she opened her main vents and dipped down into the comparative placidity of deeper water. Silent as a ghost *Upholder* stole through the mine-field charted as QB65. The mines and their mooring cables kept the asdic rating more than usually busy; his task during this passage was, perhaps; the most exacting of all, for it was incumbent on him to detect instantly any menace or impediment to safe travel. His nerve was racked to the utmost by this constant, devoted listening. Thanks in great measure to his devotion to duty, the passage was safely made, and when darkness screened the sea, *Upholder* emerged from the depths at 1927. By 2230 that same night she was west of Marettimo Island, and the seas that had proved so annoying were easing in weight and viciousness. They continued moderately, however, for quite a while, and a long swell caused the submarine to take disconcerting plunges into the deep troughs. She was a mere 630 tons and a comparative cockleshell when thrown about by the type of weather to be found off Marettimo. Up to the sleek crests she surged, poised there momentarily, then, with a racing and thrashing of propellers, dived viciously, and the din of those racing screws was shattering as they found only thin air on which to bite.

On the 4th, at 0630, when 6 miles out from Cape St. Vito, *Upholder* dived down to her usual cruising depth. By 1357 Norman had one enemy destroyer under periscope observation. He watched closely as she proceeded eastwards. Cape St. Vito is the western outpost of the Gulf of Castellammare.

'Diving stations' sounded through the hull. 'Stand by three torpedoes. Half speed ahead!' Like his famous exemplar Norman had no intention of missing any chances. Lieutenant Ruble, the American, watched the proceedings eagerly and admiringly, for the efficiency of all movements was at once apparent. Depth-keeping was extremely difficult for the swell tended to lift the submarine clear from the depths and on to the surface, where detection was inevitable.

The attack team clustered round Norman. The distance narrowed between submarine and ship. Ruble held his breath as Norman said 'Fire three!' There were three 'poshes' of air coming violently into *Upholder's* hull. Three quick shudders shook her, and for good or ill, three torpedoes streaked towards the target. And all three missed, clean-wasted effort. Just the luck of the game again, with a turbulent sea aiding the enemy, since no torpedo can be expected to run true in agitated water.

By the hydrophone effects it immediately became obvious that the hoped-for victim had sighted the torpedo-tracks. It was reduced to certainty when four minutes after the discharge of the missiles, depth-charges began to shatter *Upholder's* silent world. In the laconic entries in the log little stress is laid on these explosions: they were as much a part of the routine as the serving of meals. The hunt was on with a vengeance. Ten depth-charges blasted the area around the disappointed submarine as she crept cautiously towards a quieter, safer area of the Messina Straits.

At 1250 another vessel was picked up by hydrophone effects. It was recognised as a sub-hunting trawler, when, two minutes afterwards, seven depth-charges tore the seas astern of *Upholder* into curdled froth. These explosions caused no anxiety to men with twenty-one patrols behind them. Torpedoes were being re-loaded into the empty tubes, but a defect prevented Tube No. 3 being re-loaded.

This sporadic attack died away and by 1930 *Upholder* was free to surface again.

On 5 February, on the surface, the British submarine patrolled the convoy route between Cape Gallo and Castellammare Gulf. At 0110 'Diving stations' sounded off. The crew promptly obeyed the peremptory summons and the submarine closed in on what promised to be a valuable target. Nothing was generally known of the nature of this target until the look-out's report: it was an enemy U-boat. At once came the instruction: 'Stand by three tubes!' Men rubbed their hands – to destroy a U-boat meant saving countless British lives, much British property. Closer and closer *Upholder* crept, anticipation running high.

Lieutenant Ruble, the American, recognised the object, saying: 'It's just a rock!' And that was all it was – but at an hour or so after midnight in Stygian gloom, a bit of volcanic stone protruding from the sea can easily be mistaken for something man-made and critical. It showed that *Upholder's* look-outs weren't missing any chance of securing a bag.

Action was broken off and routine work resumed. But at 0630 that same morning when darkness still permitted surfacing, the bridge look-outs spotted two ships moving fast to the eastward, hugging the shore, as caution taught the enemy to do. Visual observation could not immediately identify them, but the asdic rating declared them to be destroyers: the pitch of their propellers giving a different registration from those of merchant ships. The early dawn-haze shrouded these strangers to some extent. Since they promised to be a distinct menace, Lieutenant Norman decided to dive forthwith, and plunged deep, five miles off Cape Gallo. The periscope was still active, however, and shortly after noon that day, Norman sighted the masts and funnels of several small craft hanging closely to the protective land.

Here was promise of action again. 'Group up! Diving stations! Half ahead!' Shudders shook the submarine as she headed nearer towards the convoy.

At 1250 word was given to raise the periscope, to reduce speed to 'slow ahead', and to group down. Up zizzed the magic eye; Norman was practically prone on the deck as he grabbed the handles, to rise with the rising instrument until its summit burst through the tumbling seas.

Between the slapping waves the enemy was identified as two small merchantmen with one destroyer ahead; something was also astern, and this was considered to be a U-boat. This was the only unit at all likely to come within range. Therefore Norman closed in, near enough to make identity certain. It wasn't a U-boat, but an Orsa-class destroyer, and it was 4,000 yards away. Two minutes after making this discovery an aircraft flew so low that its shadow practically blacked out the periscope.

So Norman ordered the instrument back to its housing, and went to a depth of 70 feet. The aircraft had spotted him and had sent its report to the destroyers; one of them turned sharply and headed directly towards *Upholder*, its asdics pinging frantically.

Down below was silence, complete and protective. Her head was pointed northwards, her motors made no sound beyond a gentle purring. At 1345 single depth-charges in the distance shook the seas, the sound-waves travelling fast and menacingly; but to such experts as those under water, it was obvious that danger was diminishing. In all eight detonations were registered. Tactical silence was continued until 1820, by which time two armed trawlers in line abreast formation passed astern, but failed to drop any charges.

At 2000: 'Diving stations. Blow main ballast' was ordered. Up went the submarine, her conning-tower hatch opened, and instantly the generators were started up, whilst volumes of invigorating air swept fore and aft. The very considerable rolling of the hull gave the crew no uncertainty about being surfaced.

At 2127, although the human eye could discern nothing beyond sea and sky, the almost superhuman hydrophone – the scientific ears – registered the rapid approach of a destroyer. Instantly the alarm button was pressed and down went the *Upholder* like a diving porpoise. It was a genuine cat-and-mouse game that was being played. The submarine reached 40 feet and levelled off. Keen ears listened. The destroyer was searching hard and relentlessly. *Upholder* was rather like a hunted hare, hardly daring to breathe. This tension endured until 2200; thirty-three minutes in actual time; an eternity to those waiting in suspense, and, for all they knew, on the brink of quick destruction. But then the H.E. faded and, taking a chance, Norman surfaced for a general look-see. All was clear.

February 6th passed without notable incident, even though distant explosions were audible. The character of these bursts couldn't be ascertained; it was assumed that some other attack was being carried out – probably on another British submarine. The final estimate was that, in this ultra-volcanic region, they were probably disturbances of that character. Anyhow, the placidity of *Upholder* was in no way disturbed.

Fifteen minutes after the date-slip 6 February had been ripped off the calendar, H.E. again reported: 'Destroyer to the northward,' but the bridge look-outs saw nothing disturbing. The generators were stilled so that listening could be more exact. Even so, nothing was spotted, though the sea was now silkily calm and sedate. Fourteen minutes later those look-outs saw flares falling on the far side of Levanzo Island, and these impromptu fireworks continued their display for the best part of an hour, by which time it was bright moonlight enough to make a poet enraptured. Lovely weather for a pleasure-cruise, but too revealing for a war-time submarine only 3 miles from Cape St. Vito. That Mediterranean moon might have been broad daylight so far as protection was concerned. Any moment *Upholder* was liable to be spotted, and spotting meant prompt attack of one sort or another. So, deeming caution the better part of safety, Norman decided to dive. It was a wise decision, for when the submarine surfaced again, air activity was already evident. By the time she dived afresh after a brief 'breathing', the sky was alive with aircraft.

Notwithstanding the risks run, the periscope constantly broke surface, searching for prey, everlastingly searching. At 1010 a tug – a small one – was sighted. She was towing an empty lighter in a westerly direction. Between 1150 and 1245 four schooners sailing west were observed, and two similar craft heading east. Then one small patrol boat showed in the field of vision – steaming resolutely up and down as if questing for a kill. And still more aircraft roared through the skies above. Ugly waters in which to manoeuvre!

Later in the day an armed trawler led four indeterminate craft, none of great size, about 90 feet in length and showing an 8-foot freeboard. These vessels carried rams for'ard, and whether or not they were a new device in submarine-hunting it was not possible to ascertain. As their speed was calculated at a mere 8 knots, it was hardly likely that such was their purpose. Nothing was to be gained by attacking such small vessels and it would mean unnecessary exposure. Lieutenant Norman refrained from any demonstration.

Thus far the patrol had not been very successful, and when *Upholder* dived after a surfaced night, at 0630, it seemed as if barren hours were to continue, for aircraft were spotted to the south'ard; that meant constant alert. At 1720, however, the periscope revealed greater promise: one destroyer and a merchantman of some 2,500 tons came into view. The locality was off Castellammare Gulf. Norman was prompt to order readiness for action after tedious waiting. It was a case of 'Diving stations! Stand by one, two and four torpedoes; half ahead both motors'. The attack had commenced and the outstanding question in the minds of all hands was: Would Lieutenant Norman do full justice to the Wanklyn tradition? He had a fantastically high standard to attain. No one dared predict, all contented themselves with hope.

At 1739 the range was 1,300 yards, and Norman gave his orders: 'Fire one, fire two, fire four!' Immediately the torpedoes were running; the control-room clock's second hand hadn't completed a full circuit when a torpedo smashed destructively through the side of the merchantman. The moment this obvious hit was recorded, *Upholder* planed down to 70 feet on an altered course that took her in a westerly direction.

Hydrophone effect of the merchant vessel was no longer apparent, an indication that she was well and truly disposed of. Down to 70 feet went *Upholder*, the asdic rating reporting 'Destroyer stopped'. So did *Upholder* stop, with 'Silent routine' quietening any commotion likely to occur. The destroyer was listening closely. So, too, was *Upholder*. Norman played Brer Fox and laid low. The destroyer made the first move, rushing in to attack at high speed. Norman rang for 'high speed' in his turn, for already the depths were being violently disturbed by a cascade of explosions, which as they thundered with shattering din, broke into hundreds of fragments which rattled like shrapnel on *Upholder's* casing. She bucked and plunged in the manner of a wild mustang. But she was well used to this uneasiness. Any experienced submariner is prepared to assert that no one ever gets really accustomed to a severe depth-charging!

The destroyer stopped again, listening hard; she speeded up and came in afresh for a new attack. *Upholder* altered course and depth afresh, with the underseas boiling frantically around her: a veritable witches' cauldron of hate and destruction. It would appear that Wanklyn's Pride – as *Upholder* might well be re-named – was condemned; her existence appeared to hang on by only the slenderest thread. These desperate depth-charges rained down at intervals between 1810 and 1825. The destroyer stopped, started afresh. *Upholder* did the same as the weird game of hide-and-seek proceeded. Norman dodged death by a series of miracles.

Then at 1830 *Upholder* was granted a reprieve. Maybe her attacker had emptied her depth-charge racks, maybe she saw herself as a sitting target for her would-be prey's torpedoes; at all events she suddenly broke off her attack, and headed eastwards at high speed – 330 revolutions, which indicated a pace in the region of 33 knots. After five minutes hydrophone effects faded and died. Assured that immediate danger was over, Norman planed up to periscope depth, to find nothing but an empty sea, and fortunately, as empty a sky. True to the Wanklyn tradition, Norman, worthy disciple, had won through a terrific ordeal. Two torpedo tubes were reloaded by 1900 and, nothing promising being indicated, the submarine surfaced at 2130.

The coming dawn of 9 February saw *Upholder* diving at 0630. A very strong wind-force had sprung up during the night, whipping up turbulent, white-crested seas that caused the tiny submarine to break surface repeatedly from periscope depth. Since this bucking and plunging was upsetting everyone, and since it rendered accurate action impossible, Norman decided to make for a lee under shelter of Cape St. Vito; but even there a heavy swell prevented the *Upholder* from remaining at constant periscope depth.

February 10th promised little better conditions for a busy submarine: there was a continuing heavy swell with violent rain-squalls and visibility was reduced to practically zero.

Consequently, on the eleventh day of the month, and undoubtedly to the relief of all hands, course was laid for home. The minefield QB65 was safely negotiated, and by the 13th, at 0720, *Upholder* was snug at her moorings in Lazaretto Creek. The patrol was satisfactorily completed.

Captain Simpson's comment on this patrol was succinct and satisfactory from a man who seldom indulged in over-praise: 'This was a well conducted operation, owing to the constant air activity.' That might be assessed in less conservative language as V.G.I. i.e., 'Very Good, Indeed.'

CHAPTER 15

SUBMARINE CONCENTRATION

IF it be true, as many sailors believe, that ships possess half-souls, *Upholder* must have quickened to more intense purposefulness when David Wanklyn again resumed command after Lieutenant Norman, who had kept the tradition going.

Wanklyn knew his boat as a skilled rider knows his mount: its possibilities and its weaknesses. When *Upholder* sailed from Malta at 2115 on 21 February 1942, she was one unit of a concentration of eight comparatively similar craft, and the object of this flotilla was to smash a very large convoy that Intelligence suggested was expected to try to reach Tripoli from the eastward.

Four submarines of this proposed concentration were already at Khoms, the other four were to join up on the 23rd.

By 10 p.m. on the 21st, Malta was already out of sight astern. *Upholder*, taking the customary surface passage precautions, was zigzagging along stereotyped lines. It wasn't a promising start; high seas were running and these lashed the tiny craft distractingly. Occasional heavier combers set her shuddering like a wounded animal. The bridge look-outs, soaked to the skin and miserable, were glad beyond expression when the approach of morning sent the submarine diving down to the calmer depths.

By nightfall, again, the weather had worsened, if that were possible. Wanklyn surfaced and fought it out with the head-seas, for he loved a scrap, whether with an enemy or the tumultuous sea. The man was a fighter – a glance at his picture is an assurance of that, and action was the breath of life to him. His look-outs hardly shared his zeal; they were subjected to many chilly drenchings, but that was part of the bitter game of sea warfare.

Those clamorous head-seas staged a problem for Wanklyn: he was being held back by the incessant buffeting and his fear was that he might be late in reaching his appointed area by dawn of the 23rd. After close observation of the conditions he decided they were not likely to improve, but risks were worth taking in the interests of punctuality. Consequently he stopped the zigzag and steered a straight course which would increase the danger of attack, but also improve his speed.

Upholder's tiny bridge was a miserable place enough; spin-drift lashed it incessantly. The seas encompassing the slender hull were black-ugly, crested with menacing foam that ran like milk in the deep troughs, for the Mediterranean can kick up as ugly weather as Cape Horn when in the mood for it. A high gale whistled around the periscope standards and jumping-wire when Wanklyn yelled down the voice-pipe above the elemental din: 'Stop zigzagging!' In the control-room the helmsman repeated the order back to the bridge to acknowledge his understanding and obedience, juggled with the wheel and set the submarine on as straight a course as conditions allowed. *Upholder* began to save mileage, but if spotted by an enemy sub. she was unquestionably a sitting duck. That was a chance which had to be taken, if punctuality were to be observed. Not that Wanklyn was a foolhardy commander by any means, but his cool, calculating and logical brain was always prepared to accept and answer a challenge if he considered it advisable. So, during the night of the 22nd and the early part of the 23rd, his command forged on resolutely, if not exactly steadily-steer the course and damn the torpedoes being the uppermost thought in the skilled tactician's brain.

Yet, despite the risks taken, and hanging on the surface long after daybreak, was not the least of them; by 0700 on the 23rd she was still 12 miles from her ordered position. When she did dive at 0700 visibility was poor, but 0810 brought along the searching eyes of the Italian Air Force; one Cant (seaplane) was observed through the periscope. Wanklyn estimated this seaplane to be part of an escort, but no convoy came into his sights.

By 0904 visibility was down to 5,000 yards. The asdic rating reported several hydrophone effects from revolving propellers, but nothing came into visible range; some fifty minutes or so later considerable depth-charging was audible, to indicate that one or other of the accompanying flotilla was getting a thorough shaking-up.

By 1000 *Upholder* had reached her allotted position, but, alas, no ships passed through Wanklyn's area, and at 2100 the submarine concentration was ordered to break up: the individual orders for *Upholder* being that from now on she must patrol the western approaches to Tripoli.

This she did, uneventfully, until 2230 on the night of the 24th of the month, when the bridge look-outs spotted two ships bearing 210 degrees – that is South 30 West, and steaming at approximately 10 knots. 'Diving stations! Full ahead!' followed automatically on the sighting, and instantly the chase was on, the distance closing quickly: 7,000 yards ... 6,000 yards ... 5,000 yards. At this range the enemy craft were identified as destroyers – special enemies of submarines – in consequence Wanklyn broke off the attack, as, weighing up the prospects, he wanted bigger game than waspish enemy killer-ships. He took a big chance by remaining surfaced and cheekily followed the destroyers towards Sidi Blal.

By dawn of the 25th, however, *Upholder* was again below the surface, seeing all and being seen by none. Only the periscope occasionally zizzed up through the creaming waters to scan the scene and estimate the prospects. At 0900 that scene was not particularly promising: nothing showed in the field beyond one small brig steering west; again, at 1210 the same brig was in the periscope view, heading back towards Tripoli. A blank day was promised – one of many, but hope did not die. Wanklyn waited for dusk before surfacing. Immediately the generators went into action to re-charge the batteries whose power propelled the submarine. Welcome fresh air gushed through the near-stifling interior; men filled their lungs in grateful relief. The look-outs kept their usual watchful alertness; hope continued to spring in their hearts. But that night was as peaceful as a desert oasis when no caravans are arriving.

At 0508 on the morning of the 26th, however, this placidity was rudely shattered by the look-outs' report that an object suspiciously like an enemy U-boat was in view. 'Night alarm' was sounded almost automatically; 'Stand by all tubes' followed. *Upholder* closed in cautiously towards the suspected U-boat, but a nearer view identified this suspicious sighting as two small destroyers – and to have attacked one would have meant instant and probably deadly retaliation. But though attack was inadvisable, watchfulness continued and, to the surprise of those penetrating eyes, a considerable carelessness on the enemy's part was observed. It seemed incredible that still lighted cigarette-ends should be tossed overboard, sparkling in the gloom like fireworks, and a complete give-away of position to any searching eyes. Doubtless David

Wanklyn wished he had a better supply of torpedoes with which to teach the casual smokers a much-needed lesson! But such munitions as *Upholder* carried were too valuable to be used on trifling targets.

By 0512 it was time to dive, as the destroyers appeared to grow suspicious. They stopped and turned their bows towards the submarine's position, listening intently. So *Upholder* slid into the protective depths.

But curiosity still prevailed in the minds of *Upholder's* crew, and by 0530 the order 'Blow main ballast. Surface!' was given. What did the apparently aimless presence of these destroyers mean exactly? It was necessary to find out, so up came the scent-hunting submarine, but only for a few breathless seconds. Within less than a minute the order to 'Dive-dive-dive' was spoken, with 'All below' as an accompaniment. The look-outs had hardly accustomed their eyes to the gloom when they were piling down the conning-tower hatch again for those two inquisitive destroyers were only 1,000 yards away! Answering the added command 'Silent routine', *Upholder* grew quiet as growing grass; only an occasional cough and the sleek swish of the single propeller-shaft broke the brooding silence. The asdic rating collected no information once the descent was completed, for both destroyers were motionless. Tension grew: men hardly dared to breathe. And when that tension became practically unbearable the submariners were aware of a new, strange sound – one that puzzled them at first by its unusualness. It was the anti-submarine transmitter sending from the two destroyers, whose suspicions were obviously aroused. In that unreal undersea world of Jules Vernean Fantasy, anything new bred added suspicion. Science might be producing new marvels to meet new emergencies and each day brought its surprises. Wanklyn knew well enough that he and his kind were the focus for ingenious experiments. He climbed into the conning-tower trunking where the sounds might be more audible and capable of skilled analysis. They had heard anti-submarine transmissions often enough before, but here was something definitely odd and disconcerting. These mysterious sounds were precisely like a rusty gate-hinge creaking as the weighty gate is opened by a determined hand. No wonder Wanklyn's hair threatened to stand on end: no wonder the famous beard bristled! What diabolical device had the enemy created?

The grating squeak continued, adding mystery to mystery. There was, however, no sudden depth-charge attack. The single propeller of *Upholder* continued its leisurely turning, as if with bated breath. The other propeller-shaft was motionless in case too much stir below might be a betrayal. Curiosity mounted in Wanklyn's probing mind. And nothing resulted! Presently the squeaking sound faded and died away. The cnystery still remains unsolved. Wanklyn gave the order 'Half ahead' and the echo was lost and apt to be forgotten except for a curt entry in the log.

At 0800 the periscope poked up for a general glance around. All that was observed were two Spica class destroyers returning to Tripoli. They didn't know they were under close observation, but being unworthy of the expenditure of ammunition, they passed on unmolested.

At 0930 another destroyer was spotted. She was heading towards *Upholder* along the swept channel from Tripoli. Wanklyn scrutinised this new intruder very carefully to recognise her as the Italian destroyer *Generale Antonia Cantore*. She was allowed to pass just as when she was again observed, at 1405, returning to Tripoli at a 20-knot gait. Wanklyn's comment was: 'No attack was made as target was unworthy of possibilities in this area.' No use trying to break open a hornets' nest, in a word!

All these seemingly commonplace details bear witness to the lynx-eyed watch kept on enemy ship movements. Little escaped observation, even if the enemy was quite unaware of the sustained vigilance. Many a living Italian would draw surprised breaths if he knew just how near to death's brink he was on countless occasions.

Dawn of the 27th found *Upholder* at periscope depth once more after a sterile night. The sea was millpond calm, and Wanklyn, always out for information likely to prove useful to the common cause, decided to reconnoitre *Zuaga*. At 0900 he was watching by periscope two minesweepers active in the searched channel. He kept them under observation as they swept as far as Marsa Sorman. Then they completed their beat and returned. But a very watchful eye was still kept on this area, noting a host of comparatively trifling details that might stand the Navy and R.A.F, in good stead on a later occasion. Such scrutiny however was checked by the blowing up of a fierce sandstorm. In many respects *Upholder* might have been trapped in the desert itself – a submarine out of her element!

The golden blast was left astern without delay as Wanklyn laid a course for Sidi Blal. Obviously there was nothing doing meantime.

Not, that is, until the asdic rating reported faint H.E. bearing 0600 degrees. This was at 1845. Instantly the periscope rose from below surface. Wanklyn pressed his eyes to the rubber eyepiece. For a lovely moment he rubbed his hands together in satisfaction. Ah, after long waiting, here was a worthwhile target: a large merchant ship, dazzle-painted to baffle any enterprising submarine likely to spot her. Escorting this vessel was one lone destroyer. Action orders followed this verification. 'Diving stations. Forty feet. Full ahead!' The boat quickened; any lethargy fled as *Upholder* closed in swiftly. 'Stand by one, two, and three torpedoes. Depth-setting 8 feet.' The whole crew came alive with eager anticipation. By way of a running commentary to interest his men, Wanklyn mentioned that the target was a 5,500-tonner, a worthwhile bag.

He added 'Group down. Slow ahead. Twenty-eight feet.' *Upholder* slowed her under-water progress. 'Up periscope.' Squatted on his haunches Wanklyn grabbed the handles and rose erect. The upper end of the instrument pierced the surface, and there, dimmed by washing water, was the picture to gladden a submariner's heart: two ships, 2,800 yards away. Big-game stalking in the African jungle was nothing to it. Suspense tautened everywhere. Hearts quickened their beat, for each attack was a new adventure, with untold possibilities. The stealthily ticking clock in the control-room showed five minutes after seven.

'Fire one!' *Upholder* shivered. Wanklyn waited for a slow fifteen seconds to pass. 'Fire two' he said. There came another shudder, another poosh of air, and fifteen more pregnant seconds ticked away. 'Fire three.' A jolt shook the submarine to indicate that all torpedoes were running. Wanklyn ordered his periscope down and a depth of 70 feet. As the instrument slid into its well – Crump! Wanklyn stood back, his immediate work completed. This was a hit without question, and fifteen seconds later another 'crump' told that a second missile had registered on target. Two certain hits!

'Good old Wanks!' sounded from various sections: honest praise of skilled craftsmanship.

Within two minutes the asdic rating reported: 'Destroyer increasing speed and coming in!' On the heels of the warning came the swishing gurgle of a pattern of depth-charges descending, and bursts of ear-splitting and terrifying din. Even these hardened veterans felt tremors of anxiety as the lights, as usual, crumpled and tinkled down to the deck. Also as usual, the wisecracks of the pretendedly indifferent crewmen mingled with the clatter. Pure bravado? Well meant, all the same; much better than blind panic. It wasn't so much the noise of that pattern of eight charges that worried the crew. You don't hear the explosions that destroy you; the mere fact of hearing tells you that you are still alive. But the apprehension of the next salvo fills the mind with new possibilities. When being hunted a submariner measures time – and life – between one burst and the next. One thing – if it came it would be quick, wellnigh painless – or would it? Philosophising doesn't help to any noticeable extent. You live in a state of suspended animation until the report comes, as it came from the sentinel at *Upholder's* asdic.

'Destroyer heading away!' And this particular destroyer was indeed doing just that – hurrying to collect survivors now floundering in the water in the spot where a few moments before a seaworthy ship had proudly steamed.

Then some few minutes later a new sound became audible to naked ears in *Upholder's* interior; a sound that needed no magnification to explain itself. It was almost exactly similar to the noise made when crushing an empty matchbox in one's hand. But it held greater significance that that: it was the tortured, riven metal of a torpedoed ship as she disintegrated.

Within five minutes or so the periscope rose for observation. Only the destroyer was in sight: stopping, moving, stopping again as she collected the survivors, watched interestedly by the eyes of the man who had accounted for it all. Twenty minutes passed thus, when the enemy ship headed away from a treacherous locality for Tripoli and safety, dropping single depth-charges as she went. It was noticed that her decks were crowded with drenched and dreary survivors, saved by the skin of their teeth. Since immediate danger had passed *Upholder* surfaced at 2030 and laid a north-easterly course. Nothing of value appearing, she dived again to re-load her tubes in readiness for further action, as to perform such loading whilst on the surface is practically impossible. The slightest roll or pitch can mean a fatal accident to men handling heavy torpedoes in limited space; but at 40 feet no motion was perceptible, so the torpedo-party carried on with the task in hand.

In *Upholder's* racks were stored a salvo of four 35-knot torpedoes, and at a conservative estimate they were at least twenty years old and dubious in quality, since high explosive deteriorates during long storage. But working from a closely besieged island like Malta, submarines had to be content with whatever the dockyard could supply, and these veteran missiles might conceivably do the work required of them. One of the tinfish was so old that the years had caused its warhead to swell to the extent that it couldn't be coaxed even to enter the tube. The missile had to be re-stowed in its rack to the accompaniment of raw cursing from its handlers. It is not to be wondered at that some torpedoes failed to find their targets, and submarine commanders were frequently baffled when they failed, after exquisite manoeuvring, to hear the dull, knocking note that signifies success!

Wanklyn's crew loaded the remaining three torpedoes into their allotted tubes, wiped sweating brows, and mumbled prayers that their labours had not been in vain – their share had been competent; the rest was in the hands of the sea-gods, or devils, depending on the point of view!

The ensuing days, until 3 March, were blank, completely fruitless, despite the most careful watchfulness. Each night Wanklyn surfaced, each dawn he dived; but no further attacks were possible, and so on 5 March *Upholder* re-entered Malta Harbour, with one additional bar displayed on her now famous Jolly Roger.

That she had acquitted herself satisfactorily was confirmed by Captain Simpson's report:

'The patrol was carried out with Wanklyn's usual precision, and resulted in the sinking of a valuable ship.'

CHAPTER 16

UPHOLDER'S
THIRD U-BOAT

AT 1930 on 14 March the Malta boom closed again behind the tireless *Upholder*, now under firm orders to intercept any sortie by Italian heavy units. This was a task after David Wanklyn's own heart: where the odds were heavily against him. It began to look as if he wouldn't have long to wait, for within three hours of the trim dive an E-boat was spotted, proceeding at high speed in a southerly direction. As often before, the screech of the klaxon pierced the submarine's interior, and the wild scramble off the bridge followed automatically. It was an old story by now, a commonplace of war-time submarining – on the surface one second and plunging deep the next. From below the surface Wanklyn, despite his uncannily clear sight, could see nothing in the darkness; the periscope was useless when night reduced visibility to nil but, though blind, *Upholder* still retained her hearing, the asdic rating functioning as an aid. H.E. was quite audible, until it thinned out and disappeared. Once the sea was clear Wanklyn surfaced and pressed on to an area where his services might best be employed.

On 16 March, around 2330, he was handed a signal by his telegraphist: it instructed him to take his submarine to a point off the port of Brindisi. Immediately course was laid for the Straits of Otranto. He was in a sense entering the lion's den and knew the risks he ran in waters seething with hostile craft. After proceeding in darkness for some six and a half hours, *Upholder* dived at 0605 on 17 March, and, moving at a leisurely 4 knots, with periscope barely showing, she slid through the underseas towards her allotted destination. Only curious fish were aware of her ghostly passing. It has been known for porpoises to follow submarines for quite considerable distances; indeed, many a submarine skipper has had the devil's own job to shake them off.

Beyond spotting two destroyers hurrying south at a 25-knot speed, nothing of interest occurred during the next few hours, and high-speed destroyers are not the best of targets. Then, at 1950 the call to 'Diving stations. Stand by to surface' was given. The main ballast was blown with a swish of compressed air passing through the air-lines. There was the inevitable swirl of bubbles on the sea's surface, and then among this turmoil, the lean dark hull of Upholder emerged. As customary, Wanklyn was first on the bridge, almost as the hatch opened; the look-outs on his heels. Nothing being visible, routine battery charging went forward. The generators roared, the motors purred, and a course was set for the searched channel leading to Brindisi itself: rail-head, in peace, for countless travellers heading to the Middle and Far East. But in 1942 Brindisi was an active warlike port. Wanklyn's periscope-his sub. having submerged as usual during daylight-detected a couple of enemy minesweepers busy about their lawful occasions, maintaining a clear channel for friendly ships. Then an unimportant sloop approached the port and entered it – unmolested.

Nothing rewarding, obviously, until at 1457 Wanklyn rapped: 'Diving stations!' and the customary excitement of impending action stirred the crew. With all torpedoes at the stand-by, up went the periscope, and the motors propelled at 'Slow ahead'. As the periscope descended after a brief, comprehensive survey, Wanklyn explained to his expectant men: 'One merchant vessel, one escort, two aircraft.' Themselves blinded they appreciated his consideration in keeping them apprised of every casual circumstance. Through that barely raised periscope, the Commander noticed that the merchantman was zig-zagging valiantly and that the screening aircraft were circling the one-ship convoy. Even so, the temptation to commence action was strong, until the thought came that, with limited resources, it was advisable to conserve supplies for bigger game. Even with the merchant craft within 3,500 yards, Wanklyn held his fire and contented himself with entering into his end-of-patrol report: 'This shot was not accepted owing to torpedo shortage.'

But when, at 1520, the vessel anchored in the outer harbour, Wanklyn was strongly tempted again to take advantage of such an obvious sitting-shot through the boom gate. He manoeuvred in order to take advantage of the situation – a tantalising one – for he knew that the boom-gate must be continually opening for small craft to enter and leave the roadstead; but even whilst such backing and filling proceeded, the expert's eyes glittered anew, as one anti-submarine vessel and one Perla class submarine came fairly into his sights. Both vessels were heading for Brindisi, unaware of the lurking menace outside. Wanklyn closed in towards the enemy sub., obviously the better prize, for to destroy it meant the possible salvation of many more British lives. Unfortunately it was out of the question to close within less than 5,000 yards distance and, as every missile was of paramount importance, the attack was broken off. Most probably that Perla-class submarine was not returning from a predatory raid but merely from exercises, with training classes aboard. *Upholder's* crew shrugged their shoulders in disappointment and continued at the ready. Various enemy craft entered the harbour during ensuing hours, all of them under close scrutiny. At 1550 a tug came in from the north-east; half an hour later there were three minesweepers in the periscope field. These were watched with infinite closeness, for to make their entry they must first cross the guarding minefield; by taking meticulous bearings and cross-checking every sinuous movement, a pretty fair idea of the course of a new searched channel was secured.

In another ten minutes or so four small brigs and schooners were seen to head towards open water. These were deemed unworthy of attention. But a steam freighter also emerged from the port, to bring hope to waiting hearts. Before she came within reasonable range, her skipper must have had a pricking in his thumbs to warn him of impending danger for, without apparent cause, he suddenly turned on his heel and hurried back into shelter.

Patient dogged waiting was rewarded, however, for in a little over half an hour 'Diving stations. Down periscope. Stand by all tubes' was ordered; all of which was obeyed with customary efficiency, to the curt commentary by the observer: 'One submarine up top, steering 185 degrees.' Hopes quickened. Up went the periscope after its quick descent. The attack began to take shape. All hands concentrated on individual tasks and the skipper was left to use his wits and skill to make undoubted success of this new venture.

'A submarine of the *Settembrini*-class' Wanklyn diagnosed. 'Carries no guns.' Likely enough she, too, was returning from a day's exercise run with trainees packed into her limited space. And a disturbed, disconsolate crowd they would have been had they known that those eagle eyes were watching their vessel's every movement! Speed and nature of zigzag were accurately checked. The speed was 12 knots.

'Set torpedoes to run at 8 feet,' ordered Wanklyn, as the target was surfaced and at full buoyancy. He watched with his customary concentration, and saw, at 1714, that the elusive zigzag was bringing the enemy submarine towards *Upholder*. Five minutes later the pattern of that zigzag brought her still more directly in the line of fire. This was enough. 'Down periscope – 50 feet!' By now the *Upholder* was directly beneath the four insignificant sailing craft that had recently come into the open – a nuisance for a stalking submarine. It was necessary to turn *Upholder* around to bring her into an attacking position. This manoeuvre was executed most brilliantly without even causing a ripple to trouble the placid water surface above, and so arouse suspicion that would result in a quick alarm being transmitted to the vulnerable *Settembrini*. Untroubled, the little sailing ships proceeded on their way, not even rocking to show disturbed water beneath them. When the periscope was raised again, the valuable target was only 550 yards away, and fairly in *Upholder's* sights.

'Fire one' came the imperturbable command. 'Spoosh' went Number one tube. Eight tense seconds passed.

'Fire two' said Wanklyn, eyes glued to the periscope. Another shiver shook *Upholder*; as it still quivered: 'Fire three' was ordered. Again, eight seconds later, 'Fire four.' Deftly handled by Number One overseeing the hydroplane controls, *Upholder* maintained a steady depth, notwithstanding the loss of balancing weight. Then a stunning crash shook *Upholder* as the first missile registered fairly on that unfortunate U-boat. She began to sink forthwith, her skin ripped open. Exactly as her conning tower dipped below the surface, now startled into scurrying foam, a second torpedo hit her fairly in the stern. Once more *Upholder* rocked to that fearful impact, but her periscope remained above surface, and through it two vast clouds of smoke, water and debris were observed, climbing high towards the sky. The action was over in little more than half a minute, even though manoeuvring had occupied quite some time, 'Down periscope' said David Wanklyn, his ambition momentarily satisfied. Perhaps he wondered how many valuable Allied lives he had conceivably saved on that 18th day of March, 1942.

As *Upholder* crept cautiously away, enemy vengeance quickened fast. Within half an hour or so Wanklyn was able to count no fewer than eleven vessels searching the area: submarine-chasers, E-boats and an assortment of other hunters. Apparently they searched for survivors, for though there was plenty of movement there was no decided attack. The submarine was able to re-load her tubes in comparative peace, after which, primed and ready for anything that might eventuate, she surfaced at 2045 and set an easterly course, hoping for a continuance of success.

Two hours were thus occupied when the instruction:'Dive-dive-dive' came from the bridge. The main vents were immediately ripped open. The submarine dropped down neatly, without fuss; look-outs performed their usual scramble, with Wanklyn bringing up the rear of that rapid, though orderly descent. Water was already seething over the conning tower as the hatch was clipped shut.

'Spotted an E-boat' explained Wanklyn, as he upped the periscope, which he drew down again immediately, since it was impossible to spot anything in the near-midnight gloom. The asdics listened hard, naturally, for the unseen but audible E-boat was keeping close company with its hoped-for quarry. For a whole tense hour this quest continued-the crew of *Upholder* expectantly awaiting the sinister crump-crump of showering depth-charges, which did not come, and the chaser moved away with its mission unfulfilled. Ten minutes after midnight the slip was torn from the calendar: a new day commenced, and *Upholder* came once more to the surface. Her batteries were by now almost flat, as opportunity for re-charging had been limited; whereupon the generators were started up at full power. The charging began without an instant of delay, for it must be remembered that a sub.'s batteries create what might be termed the lifeblood of any submersible.

It took almost six hours to complete this vital operation, but by then the batteries were carrying their full load. The interior had been swept by draughts of invigorating air and lethargy, imposed by vitiated atmosphere, had vanished as if by magic. All was well with Wanklyn and his men. Consequently, *Upholder* dived in close to the shore, in hope of discovering targets that could be engaged by gunfire, since every moment was of value. Though a minor ship deserved no torpedo, a shell could conveniently be expended here and there. Only four torpedoes remained, and these were of added value since the heavier naval units were expected in *Upholder's* area.

At 0737 the periscope was raised, and its mirrors reflected the images of one trawler and three fishing boats. Even a fishing boat can be of use to the enemy, and Wanklyn saw in these craft a menace to his continued activities. So he gave the order: 'Down periscope. Half ahead' and began to close in on the trawler. 'Diving stations. Stand by for gun action' was his following command. The gun-crew were ready, ammunition waiting to be flung into the breech. All unnecessary lights were switched off. The half-illuminated interior looked for all the world like a mess-deck after pipe-down has sounded, except for such ratings who stood at the ready with the cartridge-cases at their feet.

'Up periscope.' Wanklyn watched the little ships very closely. The trawler called for special observation; she may have been well armed, which, even if only small, could put paid to the British submarine's account. At a distance of a mere 100 yards from that ship, Wanklyn called 'Down periscope; blow main ballast. Gun-crew close up!' And those Italian trawlermen must have had the big scare of their lives when they saw a hostile submarine surface, like a blowing whale, a mere 100 yards away.

Thanks to intensive training Wanklyn was on *Upholder's* bridge and the gun-crew at action stations almost as quickly as it takes to write it.

Give Wanklyn credit for common humanitarianism. Although his own situation was precarious in the extreme, being so close to the shore, from whence might come at any moment a blast of explosive destruction, he signalled the trawler's crew to abandon ship before loosing off his first shell. He fired warning shots at the smaller craft, but these missed – probably purposely – and that gave time to the trawlermen to get over the side in haste. Four of them managed to launch and man a cobble, the rest of them standing not on the order of their going, but diving pell-mell into the sea. Once satisfied that human life was not endangered, and when within 50 yards, *Upholder's* Captain opened fire. Three shells struck the trawler, setting it handsomely ablaze. Promptly three more shells bored ugly holes on her water-line, and that spelt her finish. She went to the bottom with a trivial expenditure of ammunition.

It was time to dive under; but just as this operation was ordered, Wanklyn observed two brigs, one, towing the other. Both were very close inshore, but it was deemed unwise to give chase, as the submarine had already been surfaced for fifteen minutes in a very wasps' nest of potential danger: in broad daylight at that, and punitive aircraft could be called into action at very short notice.

Once in the comparative safety of deep water, *Upholder* sailed east, her periscope still up and observant. Through it Wanklyn watched two fishing smacks, one flying an ensign, pick up, the crew of the sunken trawler. At 1030 two aircraft were spotted flying in circles around the scene of the gun-action; a trawler joined in this search, and an anti-submarine schooner also hurried to take part in the hunt for the intruder.

When full darkness fell, at 1950, *Upholder* surfaced and completed her not unadventurous passage of the Otranto Straits. The following days drew a complete blank, apart from a few hydrophone effects which soon faded away into nothing.

On 23 March the seas were lashed into frothing fury by a fierce south-east gale. The submerged *Upholder* broke surface several times as the towering combers caught her in their giant hands and played with her like a child's toy. Even so, at 1720 heavy H.E. was heard on the hydrophones, but Wanklyn could make out nothing through the periscope. It was raining very heavily and visibility was reduced to practically nil, to say nothing of the giant wave-crests towering above the instrument.

He ordered: 'Group up. Full ahead!' none the less, well aware that in such weather there was unlikely to be any visible trail from the periscope. But the whining of the motors could quite easily be overheard by enemy listeners; that, however, was a chance which had to be taken if results were to be obtained. The submarine was shuddering throughout her length – it was noticed that she even groaned, as if in agonising pain. The specialists at the hydroplanes had the devil's own job to keep the boat submerged. The helmsman was driven nearly frantic in his endeavours to steer a straight course, for even at periscope depth *Upholder* was diving, rolling and pitching like a chip in a cauldron. Through this tumult the order 'Diving stations' rattled through the boat, followed by 'Stand by all tubes!' That sound indicated that the heavy ships for which he had saved his remaining torpedoes were within his range.

Upholder shuddered and shivered on, the water slapping around in her bilges, but despite the closest observation, Wanklyn could see nothing beyond the high-piling waves and the near-tropical rain. The indications however certainly denoted that something very big was abroad that blusterous evening.

At 1736 the Commander of *Upholder* saw something, dull shadows bearing 245 degrees, and evidently moving at the rate of 20 knots. Vague though such shadows were, they were identified as the bridge and funnels of a battleship, though the whole of the silhouette could not be seen. *Upholder* was calculated to be 4,000 yards away and all the evidence went to show that she could not avoid breaking surface in those baffling seas. However, miraculous work by the First Lieutenant and the planesmen kept the submarine at periscope depth; a feat to be understood only by such as have had the experience. Wanklyn's eyes remained glued to the periscope's eyepiece. Risking everything he instructed: 'Fire all tubes!' hoping that on this occasion he would make a kill to eclipse all his previous efforts. All imaginable odds were against success as four Mark IV 35-knot torpedoes left the tubes and sped on their way through tumultuous water that even played shuttlecock with the submarine. So what was likely to happen to the comparatively toy-like tinfish? Even relieved of that weight *Upholder* did not break surface, but as the torpedoes left Wanklyn ordered: 'Down periscope. Sixty feet.' As she levelled out, even at that depth, the vessel rolled alarmingly. Her motors were at 'Slow ahead' and 'Grouped down'. All eyes focused on such clocks as could be seen. A slow minute ticked by – and the question throughout the battered hull was 'Why? ... Why? ... Why?' had that truly luscious target to come along on a day like this when only a dimmed shadow was visible through the magic eye? Two minutes were ticked off: still nothing happened. It was realised that the luck of a Chinaman would be needed if a satisfactory hit were to be obtained. Another minute was added to the aggravating tally, and any second might, with unbelievable luck, bring the rolling reverberations of a 'crump' to indicate success. And the flock of missiles missed. Here was disappointment indeed, enough to turn Wanklyn's bile into something vitriolic. By 1746 it was certain that the desperate effort had been in vain: not a chance remained. Hydrophone effects reported then that the battleship was only at that moment crossing the torpedo tracks, the torpedoes already being lost in the unknown. Luck was with the enemy. By one of those freak chances that occasionally occur, the big fellow had zigzagged away at the moment the torpedoes were fired. Nothing to do but bite on the bullet and call down God's wrath on the weather His power had brewed up! Any further hope of completing a dashing enterprise was futile: the last torpedo had been fired. The *Upholder's* teeth were momentarily drawn.

At 2000 *Upholder* rose to the troubled surface of the rain-lashed sea. Nothing was in sight. She sent a radio call to Malta, reporting the futile attack on the unknown battleship, and a course was laid for home. Plunging, rolling, laden with discomfort everywhere, she headed towards Malta. The atmosphere within was such as only the toughest submariners can endure, and the indications go to show that the majority of this hard-wrought crew were violently seasick during most of that homeward run.

On 26 March Wanklyn tied up his command in Lazaretto Creek, her Jolly Roger flying high and defiantly. Amongst the many bars adorning that square of bunting were now three carrying a triumphant U in their centres, to tell the limited world that three U-boats were scored up to *Upholder's* credit. And her reception was commensurate with her success.

The tall, lean, black-bearded figure of David Wanklyn was first to leave the submarine – for, despite disappointments, he was victorious. Wanklyn walked leisurely ashore to hand in his report to Captain Simpson, whose comment on this twenty-fourth, penultimate patrol of H.M. submarine *Upholder* was:

'I consider that to have located a battleship and to have fired a salvo under the weather conditions experienced, reflects the greatest credit on the Commanding Officer, and shows excellent training; since to keep *Upholder* at periscope depth in such a sea is no mean achievement.'

CHAPTER 17

STILL ON PATROL

OCCASIONALLY, at the Malta Submarine Base, to say nothing of the 1st Submarine Flotilla's depot ship *Medway*, moored snugly in Alexandria Harbour, it was possible to see the khaki uniforms of the British Army. Who, the non-submarine men asked, were these rare visitors? There was almost always an air of mystery about them, and shrewd guesses were made as to the reason for their existence. Actually the strangers were men of 'Special Operations', attached to submarines; cloak-and-dagger heroes who secretly landed on enemy coasts by night from our submersibles to perform hair-raising feats of courage and ingenuity. Destroying troop and supply trains, blowing up bridges and depots: in short interfering with enemy activities in a score of fantastic ways were commonplaces to these gallant men, whose names deserve even more honour than they have gained.

Khaki battledress they may have worn, their habits may have been different from the web-footed fraternity, but to a man the submariners welcomed them as brothers in war, and entered them gladly into the Brotherhood of Submariners.

One such specialist was Captain R. Wilson, R.A. – better known to intimates, of which he had many as 'Tug' Wilson; a nickname which clings to the name as surely as 'Pincher' does to Martin, and 'Nobby' to Clarke. His soldierly figure was as well known to all submariners on the Mediterranean Station as were those of the most famous submarine commanders themselves. Slight, a live wire of energy, moustached in typical Army fashion, he was at all times prepared to perform the most fantastic feats.

During *Upholder's* rest-period, from 26 March to 6 April, 'Tug' Wilson was joyously awaiting passage home for a well-earned leave at the Malta Submarine Base. He had adequately completed many daring landings from submarines. With a great and growing record for selfless devotion to duty he had every reason to anticipate a pleasant leave notwithstanding the occasional reports reaching him of the devastation being wrought there by enemy blitzing.

Wanklyn and Wilson were intimate friends, with the link of mutual courage to bind them closely together. During this enforced period of waiting for Captain Wilson, and relaxation for Wanklyn, they indulged in the sport of fencing. Alertness of brain, eye and hand is an excellent accomplishment for men who spend their days – and nights – juggling with death.

During this leisurely interlude, neither man suspected that very soon the two were to be drawn more closely together. The only person at the Base with so much as an inkling of the fact was Captain Simpson himself.

The story became clear to Wilson when Simpson summoned him to his office, to make the request that he would effect just one more of his non-spectacular but highly effective landings before proceeding on leave. Simpson elaborated as the interview proceeded: the job was to set two agents ashore in North Africa on a specified task and, as the Army man had already made one successful landing in that area, he was undoubtedly the right man for the job. 'Tug' Wilson thought a lot, and he thought quickly – about his postponed leave to England, and about his previous experience on that same arid coast ...

There had been accumulated difficulties in that adventure. The first to come back to memory was the ordeal experienced in negotiating the boisterous surf in a frail, cranky canoe, which had capsized, spewing both himself and his companion-agent into the seething brew. Fortunately, from their point of view, it was raining heavily and, as the saturated agent left the tumbled beach to catch his train, he didn't attract any great attention.

Even so, thinking of past hazards and discomforts, Wilson decided to accept the new task. But wide experience had taught him that a folboat was far from foolproof in attempts to land secret agents. He insisted that he should tow these two agents to land on an R.A.F. rubber dinghy. Captain Simpson agreed to this and, as a consequence, H.M. submarine *Upholder* was selected for this adventure.

Why were these two top men of their different professions chosen for this purpose of setting secret agents ashore? Reason number one was that our submariners were playing such havoc with enemy supply ships that they were compelled to avail themselves of the shortest sea-routes possible; these being from Sicily to the African coast. So it was a vital necessity for Wanklyn and his fellow-submariners to have good solid information regarding the sailings of such transports to and from the African land war zone. The landed agents would watch closely and note such departures from the North African shores, and radio the invaluable information back to where it could be most usefully employed.

To lend a hand to our shore forces engaged in a bitter struggle with the ruthless enemy, our submarines maintained a shark-like watch with, as has been shown, sensational results; also supplies coming down through Italy by train to the 'toe' of the enemy country were regularly being sabotaged by men like Wilson, who himself had destroyed several trains, tracks and bridges. What with one thing and another Rommel's supplies were certainly getting full treatment! Readers of Army Commanders' autobiographies might well take note of these facts, to which adequate praise has hardly been accorded.

So on 6 April these passengers embarked on *Upholder*: the party comprising Captain Wilson and two native agents, thoroughly trained to their work. This trio was adequately provided with baggage, radio-sets for the agents, Wilson's own kit, one folboat and one R.A.F.-type dinghy.

Upholder's crew, in the Base, their steaming-bags packed, were waiting for the greatest moment of all: the sound of the coxswain's voice calling: 'Harbour stations!' They knew it would come, as inevitably as the sun had risen that morning over Malta's bomb-racked, sea-washed shores.

Twenty-four times they had heard that same order: twenty-four patrols, each one offering a fifty-fifty chance of a safe and happy return, exactly like the toss of a coin. Twenty-tour times in succession that coin had turned up in their favour. Was the twenty-fifth throw tempting Fate too far? What were their feelings as that compelling voice broke on their ears with its 'Harbour stations! All down the boat!'

It breeds a feeling almost akin to misery as a submariner walks towards this boat at the start of a fresh war patrol, for there is the trenchant moment when the familiar world is left behind: the sunshine, the civilisation, everything that goes to make life ashore a comparative dream of bliss, even though Malta was nothing more alluring than a war-battered rock.

So, with such a mixture of emotions, that *Upholder's* crew walked from Lazaretto Base, sped on their way by the resonant 'Good lucks! All the best!' from other submariners who, out of their own experience understood to the last degree.

A floating catwalk led from the shore to their now famous vessel. Their footsteps clanged as they crossed the steel casing to the open hatches. Down into the innards of their boat they descended; the hatches, all but that of the conning tower, thumped shut, the spider-clips made a secure spread as they were tightened down. The inboard lights seemed dim by contrast with the waning sunlight outside. The moment of parting was at hand.

Last of all came David Wanklyn, the six-foot-two, bearded, now almost legendary figure. Under his arm he carried a large envelope, marked 'Confidential – not to be opened until at sea.'

He climbed on to *Upholder's* casing, passed the envelope up to his First Lieutenant, already on the bridge. With the agility of a monkey he climbed the conning-tower footholds, and his long legs slid over the cowl designed to give protection from the weather, and to safeguard the bridge's occupants in turbulent seas.

The First Lieutenant saluted Wanklyn, reporting: 'All ready for sea, Sir.' Wanklyn returned the salute with the usually courteous 'Thank you, Number One', and that ended the suggestion of official formality. He looked towards the Base, returned the waves of his brother-officers. Faintly across the placid stretch of water he heard the cries of 'Good luck, David!'

Immediately the Base was forgotten, the task ahead dominated. 'Slow ahead, Port' Wanklyn ordered, and in the second following: 'Slow ahead, Starboard!' The telegraph-repeater in the motor-room spluttered sparks as the switches were rammed home. Astern the water churned; *Upholder* moved away, slowly at first, then gathered speed as she headed towards the harbour entrance and beyond to the open sea. To the observers ashore it was like the slow fade-out of a film:

Those observers returned to their various duties; *Upholder* had already vanished from their view. From now on there would be no more friendly handshakes or good wishes. From now on she was just a small lonely world, without a single friend, every man's hand against her, her hand against every man's. To all intents and purposes she was challenging the entire world.

Trim dive completed to Wanklyn's satisfaction, *Upholder* was now fighting and diving fit. After surfacing, Wanklyn, tingling again with the thrill of forthcoming adventure, opened the sealed orders down in the ward-room. What did he find in that envelope of the evening of 6 April 1942? His patrol orders stated *Upholder's* primary object was the success of the special operation to be undertaken by Captain Wilson. After the operation the Army captain was to be transferred to the submarine *Unbeaten*, west of Lampion Rock. *Upholder* was then to proceed southward and patrol the western approach routes to Tripoli.

As for her crew who were doing a patrol in a dangerous area and doing it when *Upholder* should long since have been back in England, no one will know their feelings; but they surely must' have cursed the shortage of submarines that had kept them from home, and well-deserved respite. They were growing stale from constant patrols and repeated action – for even such excitement can pall when carried to excess. But, curseful as they might be, they were, in typical lower-deck fashion, still keen to give of their best to their Captain.

Upholder pressed on, diving in the daylight hours and, during the night, her motors purred purposefully towards the billet as ordained.

On the night of 9 April the submarine blew her ballast tanks and surfaced. There was not even a sliver of moon, and it was very, very dark. Wanklyn and look-outs manned the bridge. The black sea and sky appeared to merge into one impenetrable element, with *Upholder* herself merely a darker shadow stealing silently through the general murk.

By 2300 the submarine was near enough to the shore for the meditated adventure; her propeller-shafts stopped their lazy turning and stark silence hung in a clammy shroud over that part of the world which was the arena for this typical expedition.

Noiselessly the fore-hatch was opened, and the canoe passed up to the casing, with Captain Wilson in attendance. To pass it up through the narrow hatchway, its centre had been in part collapsed; now the whole structure was stiffened by the tightening of the appropriate nuts. Next operation was to bring up the R.A.F. dinghy and settle it on the casing. All instructions were carried out in whispers, so intense was the prevailing silence. Wilson personally inflated the dinghy, which emitted a series of odd 'whooshing' sounds as the pressure entered its empty buoyancy chambers. This din was magnified by imagination into the sound of a high-explosive bomb being dropped, though most probably the crooning of the surf drowned it to possible listening ears. But all hands breathed heartfelt sighs of relief when the inflation was completed and stark silence reigned supreme.

The canoe and the dinghy were lashed together, *Upholder's* main vents were opened until she settled down deeper and the dark seas almost covered her casing. Thus both canoe and dinghy were easily launched over the side, and the two agents came through the conning-tower hatch as Wilson manoeuvred the two vessels close alongside the gun-platform. Complete with their radio sets, the two dark-skinned agents slipped quite easily from gun-platform to raft, and ensconced themselves in this precarious barque.

Captain Wilson commenced a stealthy paddling, and slowly both flimsy craft moved away from *Upholder's* shelter. Wanklyn, in a voice little above a whisper said 'Good luck, Tug – come back!' and added: 'Be careful; don't get caught in the surf again.'

Wilson paddled through that inky blackness, the weight of his tow slowing him down more than a little; but with barely a whispering drip from the paddle, these two strange craft headed shorewards. White surf created by wash of the sea in the shallows showed vaguely in the near-Satanic gloom. The sound of its jingle on the beach was almost startling to ears long used to silence. The Army man could do no more for his tow, so he cut his companions loose on the fringe of the surf and they drifted easily and safely through it, thanks to the R.A.F. dinghy's broad beam. Relieved of the weight, Wilson paddled back quite easily; his luminous compass helped him to navigate his craft towards the *Upholder*. There was no need for Wanklyn to show even a glimmer of light, for in spite of the difficulty of seeing a surfaced submarine in the black of the night, Wilson sighted the slender conning tower long before *Upholder's* look-out spotted him. When near enough for a cautious hail he shouted jestingly: 'Pongo approaching!' He paused a moment then added: 'Operation successful.' Wanklyn returned the greeting with a 'Well done, glad to see you back!' Then the time for compliments being over, he snapped to his crew 'Get the folboat stowed inboard and let's get away from here!' This ruthless pursuer of enemy vessels never used an oath to back his commands.

So the folboat was stowed away through the forehatch; *Upholder's* screws revolved and, thrusting the lark seas aside, she made off to deeper, safer waters. Forthwith the Lieutenant-Commander sent to Base this signal: 'Operation successful. Your 1315B/9th carried out.' He then steered a course to rendezvous with submarine *Unbeaten* at a position 2 miles west of the Lampion Rock. Dawn of the 10th arrived to send *Upholder* under the surface, where she proceeded at sedate 3 knots, until nightfall, when she again surfaced to head in the same direction.

During the early hours of the 11th contact was made by asdic between *Upholder* and *Unbeaten*. They closed in towards each other, the two ghostly shadows drawing nearer and nearer, until it was possible to effect recognition with the naked eye. Just a couple of vague shadows off Lampion Rock in the cold grisly hours forerunning the dawn.

What was their mission?

'Control room! Tell Captain Wilson to come up on the bridge ordered Wanklyn through the voice-pipe. That fetched the Army man up like a flash to join the submarine commander. First thing he noticed was that the sea was whipping up a little. Wanklyn expressed the opinion that the outlook wasn't any too hopeful. 'Doesn't look too good, Tug.' Then, after consideration he added: 'If you don't like it, finish the patrol with me. Shrimp Simpson will fly you home from Malta.'

In *Unbeaten* Captain Wilson saw one leg of his homeward journey; it was the tug of the Homeland that accounted for his decision. He said: 'Much as I love your company, David, I'll cross over to her and take my chances, if its all the same to you.'

That was a fateful decision: without doubt he must be the only man to sail on a submarine's last mission and leave her just before she was lost with all hands! And yet Wilson, now Lieutenant-Colonel Wilson, D.S.O., and Bar, T.D., in describing this moment of choice assured me that neither then, nor at any time during the patrol did he have any feeling that this was to be *Upholder's* last adventure.

He got his canoe up on to *Upholder's* casing, saw it safely launched with a cargo of spare gear for which *Unbeaten* had asked and, after the unemotional farewells that are taken by brave men, paddled across the tumbles of troubled water to the other submarine. When within hailing distance Wilson heard the voice of her First Lieutenant bawling to him: 'Go back, Tug, we have two feet of water in the fore-ends, and the batteries are gassing. You'll never make it to Gib.' Merely the thick-ended joke of a devil-may-care naval officer, but nevertheless *Unbeaten* was in a pretty sorry plight.

With the transfer completed the submarines parted company in the darkness: *Unbeaten* setting course for Gibraltar, *Upholder* steering southwards to patrol the western approaches to Tripoli. Consequently Captain Wilson was the last living man to exchange words with the ace-submariner of the Second World War.

Lieutenant-Colonel Wilson, himself a hero, says of David Wanklyn: 'It was an absolute delight to serve with him: He was never ruffled; he was a delightful personality who possessed the confidence and adoration of his crew. There was no one quite like Wanklyn, and it was a great honour to serve with him, no matter what the duty imposed.'

Incidentally, the North African agents landed during that final, fatal patrol, did sterling work for the Allied cause by sending back most valuable information.

During the afternoon of 12 April, three submarines were ordered by Captain (S) 10, to establish a patrol line to intercept a valuable convoy outward-bound from Tripoli: the disposition being that the three submersibles, *Upholder*, *Urge* and *Thrasher*, were to take up allotted positions early on the 15th; in the meantime each to carry on its respective pre-ordained patrol.

No one ever really knows what happens to a submarine lost in the course of her ultimate mission, unless she dies in shoal water where skilled divers can hold a sad post-mortem. And, in 1942, television was not available as in the more recent case of the lost *Afray*, to give a satisfactory diagnosis. Thus I, as an experienced submariner, can only make an assumption as to the fate of H.M. submarine *Upholder*.

H.M. submarine *Urge* heard the thumping detonations of depth-charges on 19 April. I was serving at that time on the submarine *Thrasher*, close by *Upholder* and, even without the aid of our asdic, we of *Thrasher's* crew distinctly heard the din of prolonged depth-charging. At 8.30 p.m. on the 14th, and then again at 2.30 p.m. on the 15th, *Thrasher's* asdic rating tried hard to get communication with Wanklyn's command, but failed.

What happened?

It can be only conjecture reconstructed from experience and from contemporary Italian reports later perused by the British authorities.

Upholder reached the western approaches of Tripoli, surfaced for the night for the usual task of re-charging batteries, allowing fresh air to percolate through the ship, and incidentally for the men to have a smoke. Fourteen hours without a smoke could be torture.

At dawn *Upholder* would have dived but before securing from diving stations and lowering periscope Wanklyn would have had one look around.

In the distance he would have seen something. Maybe just a heat haze.

A few minutes later another look would have shown him a sight to gladden his heart. An armada of supply ships with several destroyers weaving around them like watchful sheepdogs.

'Down periscope. Stand by all torpedoes. Full ahead. Group up.' The orders would follow one another and would be carried out with practised familiarity. *Upholder* would get to within range. 'Half ahead. Group down. Fire one, two, three, four.'

Wanklyn would watch through his periscope his four torpedoes running true, leaving four thin white wakes behind them.

'Down periscope. Sixty feet.' And an acute alteration of course to get away from the beginning of those give-away white trails.

After a few minutes Wanklyn would cautiously lift his periscope TO SEE FRAMED IN HIS MIRROR THE KNIFE-SHARP BOWS OF A TORPEDO BOAT RACING DOWN HIS TORPEDO TRACKS. A vicious waspish craft racing for the kill.

'Stop all motors. Silent routine. Stand by for depth-charges.'

Gradually the attack would build up. The asdic rating would report, three, four, five ships taking part in the attack. The depth-charges would come down in an almost endless shower, lights would flicker, would smash to smithereens.

Somewhere in the middle distance a sixth ship lay off, motionless. Constantly they would hear the ping, ping of her asdic ricocheting off *Upholder* back to the stationary listening ship. Every move *Upholder* made would be signalled to the others who would come roaring in for the kill, to deliver a mass depth-charge attack.

Upholder's crew, dazed by now would be hanging on to any part of the vessel within their reach.

Finally would come the last attack.

The exploding depth-charges which sunk them – those they would not hear.

The sea would pour in through her riven sides, she would twist and spin downwards, out of control.

It would be *Upholder's* last dive.

But her crew would know nothing of that. The last stunning explosions would have rendered them insensible as surely as a drug administered by a surgeon before an operation.

They died quickly and painlessly: they had given no quarter; they asked for none.

No marker shows where their grave is, no wreaths float above them. There they lay, the greatest of submariners and his crew closed up for diving stations – for ever.

In the immortal words of Binyon:

> They shall grow not old, as we that are left grow old:
> Age shall not weary them, nor the years condemn.
> At the going down of the sun and in the morning
> We will remember them.[*]

We will remember them in, perhaps a nobler shrine than Westminster Abbey or St. Paul's. In the waters in which they fought.

---

[*] From *For the Fallen* by Laurence Binyon.

CREW OF UPHOLDER

OFFICERS:

Lieutenant-Commander M. D. Wanklyn, R.N. (in command)
Lieutenant P. R. H. Allen, R.N.
Temporary Sub-Lieutenant J. H. Norman, R.N.V.R. ·
Lieutenant F. Ruck-Keene, R.N.

RATINGS:

Anderson, William E., Petty Officer Telegraphist: D/JXI36036
Blake, Leopold, Leading Telegraphist: P/JX142985
Board, Norman D., Engine Room Artificer, Third Class: P/MX55599
Brown, Thomas C., Able Seaman: C/JX125029
Burgoyne, Charles L., Engine Room Artificer, Second Class:
  C/MX51007
Davidson, Robert W., Acting Leading Seaman: P/JX143409
Foster, George J., Able Seaman: P/J113636
Frame, Frederick J., Acting Chief Engine Room Artificer (Ty):
  D/M38773
Gregory, Edmond, Ordinary Telegraphist: C/JX211752
Gregory, Frederick W., Stoker Petty Officer: C/KX80267
Heath, Alfred T., Acting Leading Stoker (Ty) R.F.R. C/KX75161
Hughes, Gwilym, Able Seaman: C/JX208360
Lane, Francis S., Able Seaman: D/JX208153

Martin, Frederick J., Acting Petty Officer (Ty): D/JXI34305
Miller, David Andrew, Able Seaman: D /JX164986 (late 106129)
Munday, Edward, Stoker Second Class: C/SKX1599
Newlands, Patrick, Telegraphist: P/SSX28994
Partleton, John E., Leading Seaman R.F.R.: C/J108856
Perkins, Frederick W., Leading Stoker: P/KX84691
Rowe, John, Acting Leading Stoker: P/KX84337
Saunders, Lambert, Acting Leading Seaman (Ty): D/JX147943
Self, Ernest E., Stoker, First Class: D/KX80123
Simmonds, Rex, Leading Signalman: P/J108490
Smith, George Edward, Able Seaman: D /JX203092
Smith, James, Able Seaman: C/JX208095
Swainston, John George, Petty Officer: P/JX125082
Topping, Fred, Acting Leading Stoker: P/KX84500
Turner, William R, Leading Seaman: D /J 110765

APPENDIX

SUPPLEMENT TO THE *LONDON GAZETTE*
of Friday 29 August 1941 (Tuesday 2 September 1941) came
UPHOLDER'S first awards
For skill and enterprise in successful submarine patrols:

To be a COMPANION OF THE DISTINGUISHED SERVICE
ORDER
Lieutenant-Commander Malcolm David Wanklyn, Royal Navy, H.M.S.
Upholder.

THE DISTINGUISHED SERVICE CROSS
Lieutenant Michael Lindsay Coulton Crawford, Royal Navy, H.M.S.
Upholder

THE DISTINGUISHED SERVICE MEDAL
Engine Room Artificer, Second Class, Frederick James Frame, D/
M38773, H.M.S. *Upholder*
Leading Seaman Francis, Gordon Selby, C/JXI45558, H.M.S. *Upholder*
Leading Telegraphist Gilbert Frederick Cummins, P/JX 139686, H.M.S.
Upholder
Leading Stoker Clifford Chapman, P/KX79256, H.M.S. *Upholder*

MENTION IN DESPATCHES (POSTHUMOUS)
Petty Officer James Farley Carter, D/J111443, H.M.S. *Upholder*

MENTION IN DESPATCHES

Lieutenant Christopher Holditch Read, Royal Navy, H. M.S. *Upholder*

Acting Petty Officer Telegraphist William Eric Anderson, D/JX 136036, H.M.S. *Upholder*

Able Seaman Lambcrt Saunders, D /JX 147943, H.M.S. *Upholder*

Stoker, First Class, Alfred Thomas Heath, C /KX75161, H.M.S. *Upholder*

WANKLYN'S V.C. PATROL: later the same year, the following awards were announced:

Wanklyn, D.S.O. Awarded Victoria Cross (this was the first submarine V.C. of the Second World War).

Lieutenant Brian Hugh Band. *D.S.C.* for courage, skill and resolution in successful submarine patrols.

Distinguished Service Medal

Engine Room Artificer Charles L. Burgoyne

Petty Officer John G. Swainston

Acting Leading Seaman Partleton

Mention in Despatches

Stoker Petty Officer Frederick Gregory

Leading Seaman Frederick J. Martin

Able Seaman Lambert Saunders

Telegraphist Patrick Newlands

Stoker Ernest Self

Leading Seaman William Turner

Just before *Upholder* sailed on last patrol Petty Officer F. G. Selby was rated Chief Petty Officer and was transferred to another submarine. This promotion saved his life.

AND THIS IS HEROES' DAY

This column of the *Daily Express* is dedicated today to the heroes of Britain and the Empire.

On the second anniversary of the outbreak of war there is a matchless story of human endeavour and sacrifice to be told. First in this Heroes' Day List are eleven officers and ratings of the submarine *Upholder*. The *Upholder* has been sinking Italian ships in the Mediterranean, and the eleven are rewarded for skill and enterprise in successful patrols.

Lieutenant-Commander M. D. Wanklyn gets the D.S.O., Lieutenant M. L. C. Crawford the D.S.C., Engine Room Artificer, Second Class, F. J. Frame, Leading Seaman F. G. Selby, Leading Telegraphist G. F. Cummins, and Leading Stoker C. Chapman, the D.S.M.

There are five 'mentions':

Lieutenant C. H. Read, Acting Petty Officer Telegraphist W. E. Anderson, Able Seaman Lambert Saunders, Stoker, First Class, Alfred Thomas Heath, and (posthumously) Petty Officer James Farley Carter.

Secret Kept

No other details of how these fine sailors won their decorations are released by the Admiralty.

On this Heroes' Day the *Daily Express* publishes the full supplement to the *London Gazette*.